GRAND SLAM
MORE RECIPES FROM THE BEST OF BRIDGE

FOURTH EFFORT
"TWENTIETH TIME 'ROUND"

WRITTEN AND PUBLISHED BY:

THE BEST OF BRIDGE PUBLISHING LTD.
6035 - 6TH STREET S.E.
CALGARY, ALBERTA, CANADA T2H 1L8

PRINTED IN CANADA BY CENTAX BOOKS
A DIVISION OF PW GROUP

HAND LETTERED BY NORM W. HODGINS

FOOD PHOTOGRAPHY BY SIMON CHEUNG
PORTRAIT PHOTOGRAPH BY PATRICIA HOLDEN

FOURTH EFFORT PUBLISHED SEPTEMBER, 1988

WITH THANKS TO OUR FRIENDS

OVER THE PAST TWELVE YEARS WE HAVE RECEIVED A VAST ARRAY OF LETTERS. THE FOLLOWING IS ONE WE RECEIVED THAT MORE THAN SUMS IT UP—

DEAR LADIES;
MY HUSBAND THANKS YOU FOR THE HAMBURGER SOUP.
MY CHILDREN THANK YOU FOR JAPANESE CHICKEN WINGS.
MY WEEKEND COMPANY THANK YOU FOR THE
'MAKE AHEADS' AND 'FREEZABLES'.
BUT WHEN MY HUSBAND IS SETTLED IN FRONT OF THE
T.V. AND MY CHILDREN ARE TUCKED SAFELY IN BED,
(THE WEEKEND COMPANY HAVING DECAMPED)
I THANK YOU FOR THE MARGUERITAS MUCHO GRANDE!

AND THE 'LADIES OF THE BRIDGE' THANK YOU ALL. KEEP THE LETTERS COMING—WE ALWAYS WELCOME YOUR QUESTIONS AND COMMENTS AND LOOK FORWARD TO HEARING FROM YOU.

CANADIAN CATALOGUING IN PUBLICATION DATA
MAIN ENTRY UNDER TITLE:
'GRAND SLAM'
INCLUDES INDEX
ISBN 0-9690425-4-X

1. DINNERS AND DINING   2. COOKERY   3. ENTERTAINING
I. TITLE: BEST OF BRIDGE

TX715.G62 1988   641.5'4   C88-098135-0

WE ALWAYS SAY "THIS IS OUR LAST BOOK". WE'VE SAID _THAT_ THREE TIMES, BUT WE'RE BACK AGAIN— TESTING, TASTING AND ADJUSTING OUR WAISTBANDS! WHAT IS "FOR SURE" IS OUR LOVE OF THE GOOD FOOD AND THE FRIENDSHIP WE'VE CONTINUED TO SHARE SINCE _THE BEST OF BRIDGE_ WAS CONCEIVED OVER 12 YEARS AGO.

AS WITH ANY CHILD, YOU GET LOTS OF SUGGESTIONS AS TO WHAT TO NAME IT. OUR FIRST BOOK WAS BASED ON THE FACT THAT THE BEST PART OF BRIDGE (TO US) WAS THE FOOD AT THE END OF THE EVENING. A COUPLE OF NAMES WE PLAYFULLY CONSIDERED WERE "SON OF ENJOY" OR HOW DO YOU LIKE "THE DEATH OF A BRIDGE CLUB"?

WE'VE INSTALLED REVOLVING DOORS ON OUR HOUSES. LIFE IS HECTIC—TRYING TO KEEP TRACK OF OUR DARLINGS IS NO EASY TASK. TIME IS RACING BY. WHEN WE STARTED IN 1976, WE WERE STILL TRYING TO GET OUR BABIES OUT OF DIAPERS. NOW THE GOAL IS TO LIVE THROUGH THE LAST HIGH SCHOOL GRADUATION. WE CAN'T BELIEVE THAT THIS FALL WEDDING BELLS WILL RING FOR THE ELDEST OF OUR CHILDREN— TIME TO GET OUT OUR COOKBOOKS FOR THE ONE LINERS FOR ALL THE TOASTS!

TO ANSWER THE QUESTIONS WE'RE ALWAYS ASKED: —_YES_—WE'RE ALL STILL GOOD FRIENDS; _NO_—WE'RE NOT _ALL_ DIVORCED; _YES_—WE'VE MADE MONEY (WHERE HAS IT GONE?); AND _NO_—WE DON'T PLAY BRIDGE ANYMORE!

REGARDLESS, THE YEARS HAVE NOT LESSENED OUR CONSUMING INTEREST IN CULINARY PURSUITS, AND WE HOPE OUR OFFERINGS SUIT YOUR THREE 'P's' - PALATE, POCKETBOOK AND PALS. WE WISH YOU A "GRAND SLAM" SUCCESS WITH ALL YOUR EFFORTS.

THE LADIES OF THE 'BRIDGE' -

KAREN BRIMACOMBE   HELEN MILES

LINDA JACOBSON   VAL ROBINSON

MARY KORMAN   JOAN WILSON

MARILYN LYLE

PICTURED ON COVER:

MUSSELS AND SCALLOPS IN CREAM-
PAGE 130

MIDNIGHT FRENCH TOAST

WHAT A WAY TO END THE DAY! –
AND START THE NEXT!!

1	DOZ. EGGS	
½	CUP CREAM	125 mL
½	TSP. VANILLA	2 mL
	THE ZEST FROM ONE ORANGE	
2	TBSPS. ORANGE LIQUEUR OR ORANGE JUICE	30 mL
1	LOAF FRENCH BREAD – SLICED 1" THICK	

MIX EGGS, CREAM, VANILLA, ORANGE ZEST AND LIQUEUR IN LARGE PAN WITH COVER. PLACE SLICED BREAD IN PAN, MAKING SURE SLICES ARE WELL COATED. COVER WITH LID OR PLASTIC WRAP AND LET SET OVERNIGHT IN FRIDGE.

NEXT MORNING, PLACE SLICES ON WELL GREASED COOKIE SHEET. BAKE AT 375° FOR 20 TO 25 MINUTES. SERVE WITH FRUIT OR MAPLE SYRUP. SERVES 6.

TREAT HER LIKE A THOROUGHBRED AND YOU WON'T END UP WITH A NAG!

SWISS APPLE QUICHE

FULL MARKS! YOU CAN TAKE THIS ONE TO THE BANK. MAKES 2 QUICHE.

PASTRY SHELLS -

1	CUP FLOUR	250 mL
½	CUP WHOLE WHEAT FLOUR	125 mL
1½	TSPS. SUGAR	7 mL
½	CUP BUTTER	125 mL
1	EGG YOLK	
3	TBSPS. ICE WATER	45 mL

FILLING -

3	MEDIUM TART GREEN APPLES - PEELED & FINELY CHOPPED	
8	GREEN ONIONS - THINLY SLICED	
¼	TSP. NUTMEG	1 mL
½	TSP. CURRY POWDER	2 mL
2	TBSPS. BUTTER	30 mL
4	CUPS GRATED GRUYÈRE CHEESE	1 L
1	CUP HEAVY CREAM	250 mL
4	EGGS - BEATEN LIGHTLY	
½	CUP DRY VERMOUTH OR DRY WHITE WINE	125 mL
¼	TSP. COARSELY GROUND PEPPER	1 mL

SIFT TOGETHER THE FLOURS AND SUGAR, CUT IN THE BUTTER UNTIL MIXTURE RESEMBLES COARSE MEAL. BEAT EGG YOLK WITH ICE WATER AND STIR INTO FLOUR MIXTURE UNTIL DOUGH IS FORMED, ADDING ADDITIONAL WATER, 1 TEASPOON AT A TIME, IF NEEDED.

THERE'S MORE, SEE NEXT PAGE.

SWISS APPLE QUICHE

THIS RECIPE CONTINUED FROM PAGE 8.

FORM DOUGH INTO 2 BALLS AND FLATTEN SLIGHTLY. WRAP IN WAX PAPER AND CHILL FOR 1 HOUR. PREHEAT OVEN TO 425°. ROLL OUT DOUGH ON FLOURED SURFACE. PLACE IN 2 - 9" PIE PLATES OR QUICHE PANS AND CRIMP EDGES. PRICK BOTTOM LIGHTLY WITH A FORK AND BAKE ON LOWER RACK OF OVEN FOR 15 MINUTES. CHECK - AND COVER EDGES WITH FOIL OR BROWN PAPER IF TOO BROWN. RETURN TO OVEN AND BAKE AN ADDITIONAL 5 MINUTES. REMOVE FROM OVEN AND COOL.

FILLING - PREHEAT OVEN TO 375°. COMBINE APPLES, GREEN ONIONS, NUTMEG AND CURRY. SAUTÉ IN BUTTER FOR 3 TO 5 MINUTES, OR JUST UNTIL SOFT. COOL. SPOON INTO COOLED PIE SHELLS AND TOP WITH GRATED CHEESE. COMBINE CREAM, EGGS, VERMOUTH AND PEPPER. POUR SLOWLY OVER CHEESE. TURN OVEN DOWN TO 350°. BAKE QUICHE ON MIDDLE RACK FOR 35-45 MINUTES OR UNTIL FIRM AND GOLDEN. WATCH THAT PASTRY EDGES DON'T GET TOO BROWN. COVER AGAIN IF NECESSARY. REMOVE FROM OVEN AND COOL ON A RACK FOR 15 MINUTES. SERVES 12.

IF YOU WANT TO FEEL GUILTY - CALL YOUR MOTHER.

ONCE AGAIN - IT'S AN EASY MAKE AHEAD. LOOKS FANTASTIC AND BEST OF ALL - IT'S DELICIOUS!

1 - 28 oz. CAN TOMATOES, WELL DRAINED & PRESSED		
(NO IRONING BOARD NECESSARY)		796 mL
½	TSP. BASIL	2 mL
¼	TSP. PEPPER	1 mL
1	LB. SAUSAGE MEAT	500 g
½	TSP. CHILI POWDER	2 mL
½	TSP. OREGANO	2 mL
½	TSP. BASIL	2 mL
1½	CUPS MOZZARELLA CHEESE - GRATED	375 mL
3	GREEN ONIONS - THINLY SLICED	
½	CUP RED PEPPER - FINELY CHOPPED	125 mL
2	PKGS. REFRIGERATED CRESCENT DINNER ROLLS	2 - 235 g

PREHEAT OVEN TO 350°. IN A BOWL, COMBINE TOMATOES WITH BASIL AND BLACK PEPPER. SET ASIDE. BROWN SAUSAGE MEAT, STIRRING WITH A FORK TO KEEP SEPARATED. DRAIN OFF FAT. ADD CHILI POWDER, OREGANO, BASIL, ½ CUP CHEESE, GREEN ONION AND RED PEPPER. STIR AND SET ASIDE. THE NEXT PART IS EASY!

OPEN ONE PACKAGE OF DINNER ROLLS AND UNROLL. CUT RECTANGLE OF DOUGH IN HALF ALONG THE PERFORATED LINE. MOLD HALF IN THE BOTTOM OF A 9" SPRINGFORM PAN; COVERING THE BASE COMPLETELY. PINCH TOGETHER ANY SECTIONS THAT HAVE SEPARATED.

YOU'RE NOT FINISHED YET - THERE'S MORE, NEXT PAGE.

SAUSAGE PIE

THIS RECIPE CONTINUED FROM PAGE 10

DIVIDE THE REMAINING SQUARE OF DOUGH ALONG THE PERFORATED LINES AND FIT THESE AROUND THE SIDES OF THE PAN, TRIMMING OFF ANY EDGES THAT PROJECT ABOVE TOP OF PAN. PINCH ALL SEAMS TOGETHER. SPOON SAUSAGE MIXTURE OVER DOUGH AND PRESS DOWN FIRMLY. SPREAD TOMATO MIXTURE OVER MEAT AND SPRINKLE WITH REMAINING CUP OF MOZZARELLA CHEESE. USING THE SECOND PACKAGE OF ROLLS, SEPARATE DOUGH INTO TRIANGLES AND CUT INTO $\frac{1}{2}''$ STRIPS. FORM THESE INTO A LATTICE PATTERN OVER TOP OF THE FILLING. DON'T WORRY ABOUT 'JOINS'– IT ALL BAKES TOGETHER. GENTLY ROLL THE DOUGH ALONG THE RIM DOWN TO COVER THE EDGES OF THE LATTICE STRIPS. BAKE FOR 35 TO 45 MINUTES, OR UNTIL GOLDEN BROWN. REMOVE FROM OVEN AND COOL 5 MINUTES. RUN A KNIFE AROUND THE EDGE TO LOOSEN CRUST. REMOVE FROM PAN. CUT INTO WEDGES. SERVE WITH A SALAD – SEE PICTURE, PAGE 17.

IF YOU WANT TO BE SEEN, STAND UP
IF YOU WANT TO BE HEARD, SPEAK UP
IF YOU WANT TO BE APPRECIATED – SIT DOWN & SHUT UP!

EGGS OLÉ

You'll love these—they're easy, colourful and of course—delicious! See picture, page 17.

12 eggs	
¼ cup water	50 mL
salt & pepper to taste	
3 tbsps. butter - and then —	45 mL
3 tbsps. butter	45 mL
½ to 1 cup mushrooms - sliced	125-250 mL
½ cup green onion - chopped	125 mL
½ cup green pepper - coarsely chopped	125 mL
½ sweet red pepper - coarsely chopped — (nothing's too good for your guests)	125 mL
½ cup zucchini - coarsely chopped	125 mL
½ cup tomatoes - coarsely chopped	125 mL
¼ cup green chilies (optional)	50 mL
salt and pepper to taste (again!)	
½ lb. monterey jack cheese - grated	250 g
salsa (mild or hot)	

Beat eggs and water together. Season with salt and pepper. Melt butter in frying pan and add egg mixture. <u>Scramble just until moist.</u> Place in large ovenproof dish and keep warm in 150° oven. Melt that other butter in frypan and sauté all veggies till tender. Season with salt and pepper. Spoon over eggs, sprinkle with grated cheese and return to 300° oven until cheese melts. Serve with lots of salsa. Good for 6. Caramba!!!

EGGS FLORENTINE

1	10 OZ. PKG. FROZEN CHOPPED SPINACH	300 g
2	TBSPS. BUTTER	30 mL
2	TSPS. LEMON JUICE	10 mL
1/4	TSP. CELERY SALT	1 mL
	SALT AND PEPPER TO TASTE	
2	TBSPS. FLOUR	30 mL
2	TBSPS. BUTTER	30 mL
	MORE SALT & PEPPER TO TASTE	
1	CUP MILK	250 mL
1½	TSPS. ONION - GRATED	7 mL
	PINCH NUTMEG	OUCH!
6	EGGS	
1	CUP SWISS CHEESE - GRATED	250 mL
3	ENGLISH MUFFINS - HALVED & TOASTED	

COOK SPINACH AND DRAIN WELL. SEASON WITH BUTTER, LEMON JUICE, CELERY SALT, SALT AND PEPPER. IN A DOUBLE BOILER COMBINE FLOUR, BUTTER, SALT AND PEPPER TO TASTE. ADD MILK SLOWLY; STIR AND COOK UNTIL THICK - ABOUT 10 MINUTES. ADD SAUCE, ONION AND NUTMEG TO SPINACH MIXTURE AND MIX THOROUGHLY. PLACE IN SHALLOW BAKING DISH. BREAK EGGS OVER SPINACH MIXTURE. SPRINKLE CHEESE OVER EGGS. BAKE AT 325° FOR 15 TO 20 MINUTES OR UNTIL EGGS ARE SET. SERVE ON HALVED ENGLISH MUFFINS. SERVES 6.

SAUSAGE 'N' JOHNNY CAKE

GREAT BRUNCH DISH!

16 LINK PORK SAUSAGES	
1 CUP CORNMEAL	250 mL
2 CUPS BUTTERMILK	500 mL
1⅓ CUPS FLOUR	325 mL
½ TSP. BAKING SODA	2 mL
2 TSPS. BAKING POWDER	10 mL
¼ CUP SUGAR	50 mL
½ TSP. SALT	2 mL
⅓ CUP LARD	75 mL
1 EGG	
½ TSP. VANILLA	2 mL

COOK SAUSAGES AND DRAIN FAT. ARRANGE IN PINWHEEL FASHION IN BOTTOM OF A WELL-GREASED 10" ROUND PAN. SOAK CORNMEAL IN BUTTERMILK FOR 10 MINUTES. SIFT FLOUR, SODA, BAKING POWDER, SUGAR AND SALT. CUT IN LARD TO FORM A CRUMBLY MIXTURE. BEAT EGG AND VANILLA AND STIR INTO CORNMEAL MIXTURE. ADD TO DRY INGREDIENTS, STIRRING JUST TO MOISTEN. POUR OVER SAUSAGES AND BAKE AT 400° FOR 30 MINUTES. SERVE WARM WITH BUTTER AND MAPLE SYRUP. THIS RECIPE FREEZES WELL. SERVES 8.

QUICHE LORRAINE

DON'T BELIEVE IT! MEN WILL EAT THIS!
IT'S THE DIFFERENT CRUST THAT MAKES IT.

1	9" UNBAKED PIE SHELL - FROM FROZEN PUFF PASTRY	
2	TSPS. BUTTER	10 mL
1	LARGE ONION - CHOPPED	
12	SLICES BACON - CHOPPED	
4	EGGS	
2	CUPS WHIPPING CREAM	500 mL
½	TSP. SALT	2 mL
	PINCH NUTMEG	OUCH!
	PINCH PEPPER	"
	PINCH CAYENNE PEPPER	"
1	CUP SWISS CHEESE - GRATED	250 mL

SAUTÉ ONIONS IN BUTTER UNTIL SOFT.
FRY BACON 'TIL CRISP. COMBINE EGGS, CREAM
AND SPICES. BEAT UNTIL WELL MIXED.
SPRINKLE PIE SHELL WITH BACON, ONIONS AND
CHEESE. POUR EGG MIXTURE ON TOP CAREFULLY.
BAKE AT 425° FOR 15 MINUTES. REDUCE HEAT
TO 300° AND BAKE ABOUT 40 MINUTES OR UNTIL
KNIFE INSERTED IN CENTRE COMES OUT CLEAN.
SERVES 6 TO 8.

YOU CAN'T HAVE EVERYTHING - WHERE WOULD YOU PUT IT?

THE UTMOST GRILLED CHEESE

1	LOAF FRENCH BREAD	
2	TBSPS. PREPARED MUSTARD	30 mL
1	CUP CHEDDAR CHEESE - GRATED	250 mL
1	CUP JACK CHEESE - GRATED	250 mL
1/4	CUP BUTTER OR MARGARINE - SOFTENED	50 mL
1/2	TSP. WORCESTERSHIRE	2 mL
1	EGG	
4 to 6	SLICES BACON - COOKED CRISP & CRUMBLED	
2	GREEN ONIONS - CHOPPED	

HALVE LOAF LENGTHWISE AND SPREAD CUT SIDES WITH MUSTARD. MIX CHEESES, BUTTER, WORCESTERSHIRE, EGG, BACON AND ONIONS IN A BOWL, UNTIL WELL COMBINED. SPREAD MIXTURE ON BREAD. PLACE ON A BAKING SHEET AND BROIL TILL LIGHTLY BROWNED AND PUFFED, (USUALLY 5 MINUTES). CUT INTO STRIPS AND SERVE IMMEDIATELY. GREAT FOR LUNCH OR DINNER WITH A STEAMING BOWL OF SOUP.

IT'S HARD TO SAY HOW MANY THIS SERVES — SO WE DIDN'T!

I LIKE TO DO ALL THE TALKING MYSELF. IT SAVES TIME AND PREVENTS ARGUMENTS.

PICTURED ON OVERLEAF:

EGGS OLÉ - PAGE 12

SAUSAGE PIE - PAGE 10

ASSEMBLE EARLY IN THE MORNING AND YOU'RE FREE TO ORGANIZE YOURSELF WITH LAST MINUTE DETAILS. (FRESH SEAFOOD IS BEST!)

⅓	CUP BUTTER OR MARGARINE	75 mL
⅓	CUP FLOUR	75 mL
2	TSPS. PREPARED MUSTARD	10 mL
1	TBSP. ONION - GRATED	15 mL
1	TBSP. WORCESTERSHIRE SAUCE	15 mL
½	TSP. PAPRIKA	2 mL
½	TSP. SALT	2 mL
¼	TSP. TABASCO SAUCE	1 mL
3	CUPS MILK	750 mL
1 - 6 OZ.	PKG. GRUYÈRE CHEESE - CUBED	170 g
2	CUPS MEDIUM SHRIMP	396 g
2	CUPS CRABMEAT	396 g
½	CUP RIPE OLIVES - SLICED	125 mL
1	TBSP. LEMON JUICE	15 mL

MELT BUTTER IN SAUCEPAN OVER LOW HEAT. BLEND IN FLOUR, MUSTARD, ONION, WORCESTERSHIRE, PAPRIKA, SALT AND TABASCO. GRADUALLY ADD MILK, STIRRING CONSTANTLY UNTIL THICKENED. ADD CHEESE AND STIR UNTIL MELTED. REMOVE FROM HEAT AND BLEND IN THE SEAFOOD AND OLIVES. POUR INTO LARGE CASSEROLE AND BRUSH WITH LEMON JUICE. MAY BE REFRIGERATED AT THIS POINT. BAKE AT 350° FOR 30 MINUTES, OR UNTIL BUBBLY. BEST SERVED OVER RICE, WITH ROMAINE AND PECAN SALAD - PAGE 80 AND WARM ROLLS.

BLUEBERRY BANANA BREAD

1½	CUPS FLOUR	375 mL
⅔	CUP SUGAR	150 mL
½	TSP. SALT	2 mL
2	TSPS. BAKING POWDER	10 mL
¾	CUP ROLLED OATS	175 mL
⅓	CUP OIL	75 mL
2	EGGS - SLIGHTLY BEATEN	
1	CUP MASHED BANANAS	250 mL
2	TBSPS. LEMON JUICE	30 mL
1	TBSP. GRATED LEMON RIND	15 mL
¾	CUP BLUEBERRIES (FRESH OR FROZEN)	175 mL

PREHEAT OVEN TO 350°. GREASE A 9"x 5" LOAF PAN. SIFT FLOUR, SUGAR, SALT AND BAKING POWDER TOGETHER. ADD OATS, OIL, EGGS, BANANAS, LEMON JUICE AND RIND. DO NOT OVER MIX. GENTLY FOLD IN BLUEBERRIES. POUR INTO PAN AND BAKE FOR ONE HOUR AT 350°. COOL IN PAN AND TURN OUT ONTO WIRE RACK WHEN COMPLETELY COOL. CHILL. MUCH TASTIER IF LEFT A FEW HOURS BEFORE CUTTING.

THREE RULES FOR HEALTHY TEETH:
BRUSH AFTER EVERY MEAL, SEE YOUR
DENTIST OFTEN, AND MIND YOUR OWN BUSINESS!

BEST-EVER BANANA BREAD

2 CUPS SUGAR	500 mL
1 CUP BUTTER	250 mL
6 RIPE BANANAS – MASHED (3 CUPS)	
4 EGGS – WELL BEATEN	
2½ CUPS CAKE FLOUR	625 mL
2 TSPS. BAKING SODA	10 mL
1 TSP. SALT	5 mL

PREHEAT OVEN TO 350°. WITH ELECTRIC BEATER, CREAM BUTTER AND SUGAR UNTIL LIGHT AND FLUFFY. ADD BANANAS AND EGGS AND BEAT UNTIL WELL MIXED. SIFT DRY INGREDIENTS THREE TIMES. BLEND WITH BANANA MIXTURE – BUT DO NOT OVERMIX. POUR INTO TWO LIGHTLY GREASED LOAF PANS. BAKE 45 MINUTES TO 1 HOUR; TEST FOR DONENESS. COOL ON RACK FOR 10 MINUTES BEFORE REMOVING FROM PANS. THESE FREEZE BEAUTIFULLY.

THERE ARE 3 TYPES OF PEOPLE: THOSE THAT MAKE IT HAPPEN; THOSE THAT WATCH IT HAPPEN; AND THOSE WHO SIT AROUND AND SAY —
"WHAT THE HECK'S HAPPENING?"

STRAWBERRY BREAD

3 CUPS FLOUR	750 mL
1 TSP. BAKING SODA	5 mL
1 TSP. SALT	5 mL
3 TSPS. GROUND CINNAMON	15 mL
2 CUPS WHITE SUGAR	500 mL
1 - 15 OZ. PKG. FROZEN STRAWBERRIES (THAWED)	424 mL
4 EGGS - WELL BEATEN	
1¼ CUPS OIL	300 mL
1¼ CUPS CHOPPED PECANS	300 mL

PREHEAT OVEN TO 350°. MIX DRY INGREDIENTS TOGETHER IN LARGE BOWL. MAKE A WELL IN CENTRE AND ADD STRAWBERRIES AND EGGS. ADD OIL AND PECANS. MIX THOROUGHLY. POUR BATTER INTO 2 GREASED AND FLOURED 8" x 4" x 3" LOAF PANS. BAKE AT 350° FOR ONE HOUR OR UNTIL TOOTHPICK COMES OUT CLEAN WHEN TESTED.

HAPPINESS IS WHEN YOU SEE YOUR HUSBAND'S OLD GIRLFRIEND AND SHE'S FATTER THAN YOU!

QUICK MOLASSES BROWN BREAD

1 CUP FLOUR	250 mL
1¼ TSPS. BAKING SODA	6 mL
¾ TSP. SALT	3 mL
¾ CUP FINE DRY BREAD CRUMBS	175 mL
3 TBSPS. SOFT BUTTER	45 mL
1 EGG	
1 CUP BUTTERMILK	250 mL
½ CUP MOLASSES	125 mL
½ CUP RAISINS	125 mL

SIFT FLOUR, SODA AND SALT TOGETHER. ADD BREAD CRUMBS AND MIX WELL. CUT IN BUTTER. BEAT EGG AND COMBINE WITH BUTTERMILK, MOLASSES AND RAISINS. ADD TO DRY MIXTURE. STIR JUST UNTIL BLENDED. POUR INTO A WELL GREASED ANGEL FOOD PAN. BAKE AT 400° FOR ABOUT 30 TO 35 MINUTES. TEST WITH TOOTHPICK. THIS IS VERY MOIST, AND EASY TO MAKE. SERVE WITH 'SPEEDY BAKED BEANS', PAGE 95 YOU'LL HAVE A HEARTY MEAL IN NO TIME AT ALL!! TOOT! TOOT!

A HOT LUNCH - A PEANUT BUTTER SANDWICH - STOLEN FROM ANOTHER KID'S LOCKER!

1¾ CUPS FLOUR	425 mL
1 TSP. BAKING POWDER	5 mL
½ TSP. BAKING SODA	2 mL
¼ TSP. SALT	1 mL
½ CUP BUTTER – MELTED	125 mL
8 OZ. CREAM CHEESE	250 g
2 EGGS	
¼ CUP MILK	50 mL
1 TSP. VANILLA	5 mL
¼ CUP RASPBERRY JAM	50 mL
¼ CUP BUTTER – SOFTENED	50 mL
¼ CUP FLOUR	50 mL
¼ CUP BROWN SUGAR	50 mL
1 TSP. CINNAMON	5 mL

PREHEAT OVEN TO 350°. GREASE 12 MUFFIN TINS. IN A LARGE BOWL COMBINE FLOUR, BAKING POWDER, BAKING SODA AND SALT. IN ANOTHER BOWL, CREAM TOGETHER BUTTER AND CREAM CHEESE WITH AN ELECTRIC MIXER. ADD EGGS ONE AT A TIME AND BEAT WELL AFTER EACH ADDITION. BEAT IN MILK, VANILLA AND RASPBERRY JAM. MIX WITH DRY MIXTURE AND STIR UNTIL MOIST, BUT STILL LUMPY. FILL MUFFIN TINS COMPLETELY WITH BATTER. MIX LAST FOUR INGREDIENTS UNTIL CRUMBLY AND SPRINKLE OVER TOP OF MUFFINS. BAKE 20 TO 25 MINUTES.

AH SO! AH, SO GOOD!

1½ CUPS FLOUR	375 mL
1¾ TSPS. BAKING POWDER	8 mL
½ TSP. SALT	2 mL
¼ TSP. ALLSPICE	1 mL
½ TSP. NUTMEG	2 mL
½ CUP SUGAR	125 mL
⅓ CUP MARGARINE	75 mL
1 EGG - SLIGHTLY BEATEN	
¼ CUP MILK	50 mL
1 - 8 OZ. TIN MANDARIN ORANGES - RESERVE JUICE	250 mL

TOPPING:

¼ CUP MELTED BUTTER	50 mL
¼ CUP SUGAR	50 mL
½ TSP. CINNAMON	2 mL

SIFT FLOUR WITH OTHER DRY INGREDIENTS. CUT IN MARGARINE. COMBINE EGG, MILK AND JUICE; ADD ALL AT ONCE TO DRY INGREDIENTS; MIXING ONLY UNTIL MOISTENED. FOLD IN ORANGES. FILL GREASED MUFFIN TINS ¾ FULL. BAKE AT 350° FOR 20 TO 25 MINUTES. REMOVE FROM MUFFIN TINS WHILE STILL WARM. DIP TOPS IN MELTED BUTTER AND SUGAR-CINNAMON MIXTURE. MAKES 12 LARGE MUFFINS.

PHANTOM RHUBARB MUFFINS

WHAT DO YOU MEAN THEY'RE ALL GONE? - AGAIN?

½ CUP SOUR CREAM	125 mL
¼ CUP VEGETABLE OIL	50 mL
1 LARGE EGG	
1⅓ CUPS FLOUR	325 mL
1 CUP DICED RHUBARB	250 mL
⅔ CUP BROWN SUGAR	150 mL
½ TSP. BAKING SODA	2 mL
¼ TSP. SALT	1 mL

BLEND TOGETHER SOUR CREAM, OIL AND EGG. SET ASIDE. IN ANOTHER BOWL, STIR REMAINING INGREDIENTS TOGETHER AND COMBINE WITH FIRST MIXTURE. MIX JUST UNTIL MOISTENED. FILL 12 LARGE MUFFINS CUPS ⅔ FULL.

THE TOPPING:

¼ CUP BROWN SUGAR	50 mL
¼ CUP CHOPPED NUTS	50 mL
½ TSP. CINNAMON	2 mL
2 TSPS. MELTED BUTTER	10 mL

COMBINE INGREDIENTS AND SPOON ON EACH MUFFIN. BAKE AT 350° FOR 25 TO 30 MINUTES.

AGE IS A HIGH PRICE TO PAY FOR MATURITY.

CARROT and RAISIN MUFFINS

1	CUP FLOUR	250 mL
½	CUP WHOLE WHEAT FLOUR	125 mL
2	TSPS. BAKING POWDER	10 mL
½	TSP. SALT	2 mL
½	TSP. CINNAMON	2 mL
¼	TSP. NUTMEG	1 mL
½	CUP BROWN SUGAR	125 mL
1	EGG	
½	CUP MILK	125 mL
⅓	CUP VEGETABLE OIL	75 mL
1	CUP CARROTS - PEELED & GRATED	250 mL
½	CUP RAISINS	125 mL

GREASE MUFFIN TINS. PREHEAT OVEN TO 400°. COMBINE DRY INGREDIENTS IN LARGE BOWL. BEAT TOGETHER EGG, MILK AND OIL. POUR INTO DRY INGREDIENTS. STIR JUST UNTIL INGREDIENTS ARE MOIST. FOLD IN RAISINS AND CARROTS. FILL TINS ⅔ FULL. BAKE AT 400° FOR ABOUT 20 MINUTES. MAKES 12. SERVE WITH ORANGE BUTTER.

ORANGE BUTTER:

½	CUP SOFT BUTTER	125 mL
¼	CUP SIFTED ICING SUGAR	50 mL
1½	TBSPS. GRATED ORANGE RIND	25 mL

CREAM BUTTER UNTIL FLUFFY. BEAT IN SUGAR AND ORANGE RIND.

CHEESE AND BACON MUFFINS

TASTY WHEN SERVED WITH SCRAMBLED EGGS.

1½	CUPS FLOUR	375 mL
½	CUP CORNMEAL	125 mL
1	TBSP. BAKING POWDER	15 mL
½	TSP. SALT	2 mL
½	TSP. CAYENNE	2 mL
2	CUPS GRATED 'OLD' CHEDDAR CHEESE	500 mL
8	STRIPS BACON (SAVE DRIPPINGS)	
1	LARGE EGG	
1	CUP MILK	250 mL
3	TBSPS. MELTED BUTTER... AND	45 mL
2	TBSPS. BACON DRIPPINGS... TO MAKE ¼ CUP	30 mL
⅓	CUP COARSLEY GRATED CHEDDAR	75 mL

COOK AND DRAIN BACON, RESERVING AT LEAST 2 TBSPS. DRIPPINGS. CRUMBLE BACON. COMBINE FLOUR, CORNMEAL, BAKING POWDER, SALT, CAYENNE, CHEESE AND CRUMBLED BACON (THE FIRST 7 INGREDIENTS). MELT BUTTER AND ADD TO RESERVED BACON DRIPPINGS. IN MEDIUM BOWL BEAT EGG LIGHTLY AND MIX IN MILK AND BUTTER/BACON MIXTURE. ADD TO FIRST 7 INGREDIENTS AND STIR THOROUGHLY. FILL MUFFIN CUPS ¾ FULL. SPRINKLE 1 TBSP. CHEESE ON EACH. BAKE AT 425° FOR 20 MINUTES. MAKES APPROXIMATELY 18 MEDIUM-SIZED MUFFINS.

BANANA MUFFINS

VERY MOIST. GREAT FOR THE LUNCH BOX!

½ CUP MARGARINE	125 mL
1 CUP SUGAR	250 mL
2 EGGS	
1 CUP RIPE BANANAS - MASHED	250 mL
1½ CUPS SIFTED FLOUR	375 mL
1 TSP. NUTMEG	5 mL
1 TSP. BAKING SODA	5 mL
2 TSPS. HOT WATER	10 mL
1 TSP. VANILLA	5 mL

CREAM MARGARINE AND SUGAR. ADD EGGS AND BANANAS. MIX WELL. STIR IN FLOUR AND NUTMEG. DISSOLVE SODA IN HOT WATER, ADD TO BANANA MIXTURE. STIR IN VANILLA. FILL GREASED MUFFIN TINS ½ FULL. BAKE AT 350° FOR APPROXIMATELY 20 MINUTES OR UNTIL GOLDEN BROWN. MAKES 24 MEDIUM MUFFINS.

WHEN YOU SEE A LIGHT AT THE END OF THE TUNNEL, IT MEANS THERE'S A TRAIN HEADED YOUR WAY.

HEALTH NUT MUFFINS

1½ CUPS VERY HOT WATER	375 mL
¼ CUP MOLASSES	50 mL
½ CUP ALL BRAN	125 mL
½ CUP ROLLED OATS	125 mL
3 TBSPS. WHITE SUGAR	45 mL
3 TBSPS. BROWN SUGAR	45 mL
¾ CUP WHOLE WHEAT FLOUR	175 mL
½ CUP SKIM MILK POWDER	125 mL
3 TBSPS. WHEAT GERM	45 mL
1 TSP. BAKING POWDER	5 mL
½ TSP. BAKING SODA	2 mL
1½ TSP. SALT	7 mL
⅓ CUP OIL	75 mL
2 LARGE EGGS	
2 TSPS. VANILLA	10 mL
½ CUP WALNUTS - CHOPPED	125 mL
½ CUP SUNFLOWER SEEDS (OPTIONAL)	125 mL
1 CUP RAISINS	250 mL
½ CUP DATES - CHOPPED	125 mL
½ CUP DRIED APRICOTS - CHOPPED	125 mL
½ CUP COCONUT (OPTIONAL)	125 mL

THAT'S WHAT YOU NEED. FOR METHOD SEE PAGE 31.

HEALTH NUT MUFFINS

THIS RECIPE CONTINUED FROM PAGE 30.

IN A LARGE BOWL COMBINE WATER AND MOLASSES. ADD BRAN AND OATS AND SOAK 15 MINUTES. MEANWHILE, IN ANOTHER BOWL COMBINE SUGARS, FLOUR, SKIM MILK POWDER, WHEAT GERM, BAKING POWDER, BAKING SODA AND SALT. TO THE SOAKED BRAN AND OATS-BEAT IN OIL, EGGS, AND VANILLA. ADD DRY INGREDIENTS AND COMBINE THOROUGHLY. STIR IN NUTS AND FRUITS. BAKE AT 350° FOR 20 TO 25 MINUTES. REMOVE FROM OVEN-COOL ON CAKE RACKS. MAKES 3 DOZEN.

PITA TOASTS

¾ CUP BUTTER		175 mL
2 TBSPS. PARSLEY – MINCED		30 mL
1 TBSP. CHIVES – SNIPPED		15 mL
1 TBSP. LEMON JUICE		15 mL
1 LARGE CLOVE GARLIC - CRUSHED & MINCED		
6 PITA ROUNDS		

IN A BOWL, CREAM TOGETHER FIRST FIVE INGREDIENTS, COVER AND SET ASIDE FOR AT LEAST ONE HOUR. CUT PITA ROUNDS INTO 4 WEDGES AND SEPARATE LAYERS. SPREAD EACH PIECE WITH SOME OF THE BUTTER MIXTURE. ARRANGE THE PITA ON A LARGE BAKING SHEET IN ONE LAYER AND BAKE IN TOP HALF OF PREHEATED 450° OVEN FOR 5 MINUTES, OR UNTIL LIGHTLY BROWN AND CRISP. MAKES 48 TOASTS. SERVE IN PLACE OF GARLIC TOAST OR ROLLS.

DRESSED-UP FRENCH BREAD

1 - 14 OZ. TIN PITTED RIPE OLIVES — DRAINED & CHOPPED	398 mL
1 CUP MARGARINE	250 mL
4 GREEN ONIONS - CHOPPED	
½ TSP. GARLIC SALT	2 mL
½ TSP. OREGANO	2 mL
PAPRIKA	
PARMESAN CHEESE - GRATED	
1 LOAF FRENCH BREAD - UNSLICED	

CUT LOAF IN HALF LENGTHWISE. LAY FLAT. MIX FIRST 5 INGREDIENTS AND SPREAD ON LOAF HALVES. COVER WITH CHEESE AND SPRINKLE WITH PAPRIKA. WRAP IN FOIL AND BAKE AT 325° FOR 10 TO 20 MINUTES.

HOW CHEESY DO YOU WANT IT!

1 LOAF FROZEN BREAD DOUGH, THAWED UNTIL SLICEABLE (APPROX. 1 HOUR).	
¼ CUP BUTTER - MELTED	50 mL
1 TO 2 CUPS CHEDDAR CHEESE - GRATED	250-500 mL
(PARMESAN WORKS TOO)	

CUT LOAF INTO 10-12 PIECES. DIP BOTH SIDES IN BUTTER, THEN CHEESE. ARRANGE IN BUNDT PAN. LET RISE 2 TO 3 HOURS. BAKE 20 MINUTES AT 375°. IF MAKING THE NIGHT BEFORE, COVER BUNDT PAN WITH DAMP TEATOWEL AND BAKE WHEN READY. TO SERVE - PULL APART AND PUT IN A BREAD BASKET.

WELSH CAKES

WE DISCOVERED THESE WHILST CELEBRATING ROYAL WEDDINGS! INVITE YOUR FRIENDS TO TEA.

1½	CUPS FLOUR	375 mL
½	TSP. SALT	2 mL
½	TSP. BAKING POWDER	2 mL
½	CUP SUGAR	125 mL
1	TSP. NUTMEG	5 mL
½	CUP BUTTER	125 mL
1	EGG	
2	TBSPS. ORANGE JUICE (OR LESS)	30 mL
½	CUP CURRANTS	125 mL

SIFT DRY INGREDIENTS. CUT IN BUTTER TO A MEALY TEXTURE. ADD EGG AND MIX. ADD ENOUGH ORANGE JUICE TO BIND DOUGH TOGETHER. ADD CURRANTS AND MIX WELL. ROLL TO ¼" THICKNESS AND CUT CAKES WITH 3" COOKIE CUTTER (OR AN INVERTED GLASS). COOK IN GREASED FRYPAN ON MEDIUM HEAT TILL LIGHTLY BROWNED (3 TO 4 MINUTES EACH SIDE). MAKES ABOUT 20.

TO BE NATURAL IS SUCH A DIFFICULT POSE TO KEEP UP!

TEA SCONES

TRADITIONAL AT HIGH TEA.

3	CUPS FLOUR	750 mL
½	CUP SUGAR	125 mL
4	TSPS. BAKING POWDER	20 mL
½	TSP. SALT	2 mL
½	CUP MARGARINE	125 mL
1	TBSP. ORANGE OR LEMON RIND	15 mL
½	CUP RAISINS OR CURRANTS	125 mL
2	EGGS	
	MILK	

MIX FLOUR, SUGAR, BAKING POWDER AND SALT TOGETHER. CUT IN MARGARINE TO MAKE A CRUMB-LIKE MIXTURE. STIR IN ORANGE RIND AND RAISINS. BEAT EGGS IN A ONE CUP MEASURING CUP. FILL UP TO 1 CUP MEASURE WITH MILK. STIR LIGHTLY INTO DRY MIXTURE, TO FORM A SOFT DOUGH. ROLL OUT DOUGH TO ½" THICKNESS. CUT IN ROUNDS WITH A CUTTER. PLACE ON LIGHTLY GREASED COOKIE SHEET. BAKE AT 450° FOR 15 MINUTES. SERVE WITH BUTTER AND STRAWBERRY JAM.

THERE'S NO FOOL LIKE AN OLD FOOL —
YOU CAN'T BEAT EXPERIENCE!

PICK THIS ONE – IT'S EASIER THAN TRYING TO PICK ANYTHING ELSE – A ROSE, A MAN, A DRESS...

10 to 12 GREEN TOMATOES	
6 MEDIUM GREEN PEPPERS	
6 MEDIUM RED PEPPERS	
4 MEDIUM ONIONS	
6 CUPS VINEGAR	1.5 L
3½ CUPS SUGAR	875 mL
¼ CUP MUSTARD SEED	50 mL
¼ CUP SALT	50 mL
1 TBSP. CELERY SEED	15 mL
2 TSPS. ALLSPICE	10 mL
1 TSP. CINNAMON	5 mL

GRIND OR FINELY CHOP ALL VEGETABLES AND PLACE IN A LARGE KETTLE. ADD 4 CUPS VINEGAR AND BRING MIXTURE TO A FULL BOIL OVER HIGH HEAT. REDUCE HEAT AND SIMMER FOR 30 MINUTES, STIRRING OCCASIONALLY. DRAIN. PREPARE STERILIZED JARS. STIR REMAINING 2 CUPS VINEGAR AND REMAINING INGREDIENTS INTO DRAINED VEGETABLES IN POT. BRING MIXTURE TO BOIL OVER HIGH HEAT; SIMMER FOR 3 MINUTES. PUT INTO STERILIZED JARS AND SEAL. PROCESS 5 MINUTES (SEE PROCESSING METHOD, PAGE 37 REMOVE JARS AND ALLOW TO COOL.) MAKES ABOUT 9 – 12 OZ. JARS.

PEANUT SAUCE

TRY THIS WITH PORK ROAST OR WITH ANY
MEAT FONDUE, OR SATÉ (SEE "ENJOY!", PAGE 129)

1	MEDIUM ONION - FINELY CHOPPED	
½	TSP. GARLIC - CRUSHED	2 mL
½	TSP. RED PEPPER FLAKES	2 mL
6	TBSPS. SOYA SAUCE	90 mL
4	TBSPS. SHERRY	60 mL
¼	TSP. GROUND GINGER	1 mL
¾	CUP SMOOTH PEANUT BUTTER	175 mL
1	CUP CHICKEN STOCK	250 mL
1	CUP WHIPPING CREAM	250 mL

SAUTÉ ONION, GARLIC AND RED PEPPER. ADD
ALL OTHER INGREDIENTS <u>EXCEPT</u> CREAM.
BRING TO BOIL, THEN SIMMER 30 MINUTES.
STRAIN MIXTURE, COOL, DRAIN EXCESS OIL, AND
ADD CREAM. REHEAT TO SERVE. MAKES 3 CUPS.

SOME OF US TREAT OUR BODIES
AS IF WE HAD A SPARE IN THE TRUNK.

MAKES ABOUT 8 SMALL JARS - AND THE RELISH ISN'T BAD EITHER!

6 CUPS CORN KERNELS (FROZEN)	1.5 L
3 MEDIUM ONIONS - FINELY CHOPPED	
1 RED PEPPER - FINELY CHOPPED	
1 GREEN PEPPER - FINELY CHOPPED	
½ CUP CELERY - FINELY CHOPPED	125 mL
2 CUPS CIDER VINEGAR	500 mL
1 CUP SUGAR	250 mL
2 TBSPS. PICKLING SALT	30 mL
2 TBSPS. DRY MUSTARD	30 mL
½ TSP. CELERY SEEDS	2 mL
¼ TSP. TURMERIC	1 mL
¼ TSP. PEPPER	1 mL

COMBINE ALL INGREDIENTS IN LARGE DUTCH OVEN. BRING TO BOIL; REDUCE HEAT AND SIMMER, UNCOVERED, FOR 30 MINUTES. STIR OCCASIONALLY. SPOON INTO STERILIZED JARS, LEAVING ½" AT TOP AND SEAL.

TO PROCESS: PLACE JARS ON RACK IN 3" OF WATER IN LARGE, DEEP POT. LIDS SHOULD BE LOOSE. COVER POT AND BRING WATER TO BOIL. SIMMER 15 MINUTES. LET COOL AND TIGHTEN LIDS. STORE IN COOL PLACE.

GREEN TOMATO MARMALADE

15 TO 20 GREEN TOMATOES (ABOUT 4 LBS.)	2 kg
8 CUPS WHITE SUGAR	2 kg
3 LEMONS	
2 CUPS WALNUTS - CHOPPED	500 g

WASH TOMATOES AND CHOP FINELY. ADD SUGAR AND LET STAND OVERNIGHT. CUT THE LEMONS, RIND AND ALL, INTO FINE PIECES AND REMOVE SEEDS. PUT TOMATOES AND SUGAR INTO A LARGE PRESERVING KETTLE AND HEAT TO BOILING. ADD LEMON. REDUCE HEAT AND SIMMER FOR 45 TO 50 MINUTES OR UNTIL THICK; ADD WALNUTS FIVE MINUTES BEFORE REMOVING FROM HEAT. LADLE HOT MARMALADE INTO STERILIZED JARS AND SEAL. YIELD: 10-8 oz. JARS.

GOURMET CRANBERRY SAUCE

YOUR FRIENDS WOULD LOVE A JAR FOR CHRISTMAS.

3 CUPS FRESH OR FROZEN CRANBERRIES	750 mL
1 ORANGE - CUT IN QUARTERS	
1 CUP BERRY SUGAR	250 mL
¼ CUP GRAND MARNIER	50 mL

CHOP CRANBERRIES AND ORANGE IN BLENDER OR FOOD PROCESSOR. ADD BERRY SUGAR AND GRAND MARNIER. FINI!

CRANBERRY STUFFING

GREAT IN THE CENTRE OF A CROWN ROAST OF PORK - OR IN THE MIDDLE OF YOUR TURKEY!

1/4	CUP BUTTER	50 mL
1	MEDIUM ONION - CHOPPED	
1/2	CUP CELERY - CHOPPED	125 mL
4	CUPS BREAD CRUMBS	1 L
1	TSP. SALT	5 mL
1/2	TSP. POULTRY SEASONING	2 mL
1/8	TSP. PEPPER	.5 mL
1	CUP CRANBERRIES - FRESH OR FROZEN & THAWED	250 mL
2	CUPS APPLES - PEELED, SLICED & SPRINKLED WITH LEMON	500 mL

MELT BUTTER IN FRYPAN; ADD ONIONS AND CELERY AND SAUTÉ. COMBINE NEXT 4 INGREDIENTS. ADD TO ONION MIXTURE. STIR IN CRANBERRIES AND APPLES. STUFF!

IT'S ALWAYS GOOD TO LEND A SYMPATHETIC EAR, BUT SOMETIMES IT'S HARD TO GET IT BACK!

TERRIFIC TURKEY STUFFING

FINALLY SOMETHING THAT'S <u>GOOD</u> FOR YOUR CAVITIES!

3	CUPS COOKED RICE (WILD RICE IS A REAL TREAT)	750 mL
2	CUPS FRESH BREADCRUMBS	500 mL
1	LB. BULK PORK SAUSAGE	500 g
2	STALKS CELERY - FINELY CHOPPED	
1	MEDIUM ONION - FINELY CHOPPED	
	SALT & PEPPER, TO TASTE	
1 TO 2 TSP.	SAGE (OPTIONAL)	5-10 mL

PLACE COOKED RICE AND BREADCRUMBS IN A LARGE BOWL. FRY SAUSAGE, CELERY AND ONION TILL SAUSAGE IS BROWN AND CRUMBLE. DRAIN AND REMOVE TO RICE MIXTURE. ADD SEASONINGS AND TOSS. MIXTURE SHOULD BE MOIST BUT NOT STICKY. ADD MORE BREADCRUMBS IF NECESSARY. SPOON BUT <u>DON'T PACK</u> INTO BOTH CAVITIES OF TURKEY. ANY EXTRA CAN BE COOKED IN A SMALL COVERED CASSEROLE DISH.

IT'S NOT AS EASY AS PEOPLE THINK TO GET A PARKING TICKET. FIRST, YOU HAVE TO FIND SOMEWHERE TO PARK!

SEASONED FLOUR

A FLAVOURFUL COMPLEMENT TO ANY MEAT THAT REQUIRES "FLOURING". STORE IN A PLASTIC CONTAINER ET VOILÀ! - YOU'RE ORGANIZED!

2 CUPS FLOUR	500 mL
1 TO 2 TBSP. SALT	15 - 30 mL
1 TBSP. CELERY SALT	15 mL
1 TBSP. PEPPER	15 mL
2 TBSPS. DRY MUSTARD	30 mL
4 TBSPS. PAPRIKA	60 mL
2 TBSPS. GARLIC SALT	30 mL
1 TSP. GINGER	5 mL
½ TSP. THYME	2 mL
½ TSP. BASIL	2 mL
½ TSP. OREGANO	2 mL

SALT SUBSTITUTE

1 TBSP. DRY MUSTARD	15 mL
1 TBSP. GARLIC POWDER	15 mL
1 TBSP. ONION POWDER	15 mL
1 TBSP. PAPRIKA	15 mL
1½ TSPS. PEPPER OR CAYENNE	7 mL
1 TSP. BASIL	5 mL
1 TSP. THYME	5 mL

COMBINE INGREDIENTS WELL AND PLACE IN A SHAKER JAR. IF YOU CAN'T HAVE SALT, THIS ADDS FLAVOUR TO YOUR LIFE!

GLØGG

OUR DANISH FRIEND SERVES THIS WONDERFUL SPICED WINE AT SKATING PARTIES.

1 - 26 OZ. BOTTLE RED WINE	750 mL
1 CUP BRANDY	250 mL
1 - 12 OZ. BOTTLE BEER	355 mL
1 ORANGE - THINLY SLICED WITH RIND ON	
1 SLICE LEMON	
3/4 CUP SUGAR	175 mL
3 CINNAMON STICKS	
1 TBSP. WHOLE CLOVES	15 mL
1 CUP RAISINS	250 mL
1/3 CUP SLIVERED ALMONDS	75 mL

MAKE A SPICE BAG WITH CINNAMON AND CLOVES. COMBINE EVERYTHING IN LARGE POT; BRING TO A BOIL; SIMMER FOR 1 1/2 HOURS COVERED. REMOVE ORANGE AND LEMON SLICES AND SPICE BAG BEFORE SERVING.

THE CLOSEST TO PERFECTION A PERSON EVER COMES IS WHEN HE FILLS OUT A JOB APPLICATION.

HOT BUTTERED RUM

1	LB. BUTTER	500 g
3½	CUPS ICING SUGAR	875 mL
2	CUPS BROWN SUGAR	500 mL
1	QT. VANILLA ICE CREAM	1 L
1½	TSPS. CINNAMON	7 mL
½	TSP. ALLSPICE	2 mL

SOFTEN ICE CREAM AND BLEND IN ALL OTHER INGREDIENTS. STORE IN FREEZER.

TO ENJOY: ONE SERVING.

1½	TBSPS. BUTTER MIXTURE	22 mL
1½	OZ. DARK RUM	45 mL
	BOILING WATER	

ADD EVERYTHING TO A CUP. GO TO IT BUSTER!

FUZZY NAVELS

HAIR ON YA!

9	OZ. PEACH SCHNAPPS	275 mL
3	OZ. VODKA	75 mL
2	CUPS ORANGE JUICE	500 mL
8	ICE CUBES	

COMBINE ALL INGREDIENTS IN A BLENDER. HURRY AND BLEND UNTIL FROTHY. SERVES 6. THAT'S HOW WE SPELL RELIEF.

LONG ISLAND ICED TEA

HIGH TEA! WITH A LITTLE HELP FROM YOUR FRIENDS!

3 OZ. VODKA	85 mL
3 OZ. GIN	85 mL
3 OZ. TEQUILA	85 mL
3 OZ. SOUTHERN COMFORT	85 mL
1 - 12 OZ. CAN COKE	355 mL
1 - 12 OZ. CAN SODA WATER	355 mL
½ CUP LIME CORDIAL	125 mL

MIX ALL INGREDIENTS IN A LARGE PITCHER AND FILL WITH ICE CUBES. STIR - DRINK - ENJOY! SERVES 6.

A REAL SMOOTHIE

LOW CAL AND HEALTHY - BUT IT TASTES LIKE YOU'RE CHEATING.

1 BANANA	
½ CUP APPLE OR ORANGE JUICE	125 mL
½ CUP FROZEN BLUEBERRIES - THAWED	125 mL
¾ CUP YOGURT, PLAIN	175 mL
½ TSP. VANILLA	2 mL

BLENDERIZE. MAKES 2 DELICIOUS GLASSES FULL.

NUTS AND BOLTS

FOR THOSE WHO ARE MECHANICALLY DECLINED! —
—AND JUST ABOUT ANYONE ELSE!

1	LB. BUTTER	454 g
2	TBSPS. WORCESTERSHIRE SAUCE	30 mL
1	TBSP. GARLIC POWDER	15 mL
1½	TSPS. ONION SALT	7 mL
1½	TSPS. CELERY SALT	7 mL
4	CUPS 'CHEERIOS'	1 L
4	CUPS 'LIFE' CEREAL	1 L
4	CUPS 'SHREDDIES' OR 'WHEAT CHEX'	1 L
2	BOXES PRETZELS	
2	CUPS PEANUTS (SALTED; IF YOU INSIST)	500 mL
1	BOX 'BUGLES'	
1	BOX CHEESE NIPS OR CHEESE BITES	

HEAT OVEN TO 250°. PLACE BUTTER IN VERY LARGE ROASTER AND PUT IN OVEN TO MELT BUTTER WHILE OVEN IS PREHEATING. ADD ALL INGREDIENTS AND STIR WELL TO COAT EVENLY WITH BUTTER. BAKE FOR 1½ HOURS. STIR EVERY ½ HOUR.

IT'S EASY TO IDENTIFY PEOPLE WHO CAN'T COUNT TO 10. THEY'RE IN FRONT OF YOU IN THE MARKET EXPRESS LANE.

RAREBIT IN A HOLE

A CHEESY BEER FONDUE IN A HOLLOWED OUT LOAF
- UNREAL!

2½ CUPS CHEDDAR CHEESE - GRATED	625 mL
¼ CUP SOUR CREAM	50 mL
1 TO 2 CLOVES GARLIC - CHOPPED	
2 TSPS. WORCESTERSHIRE SAUCE	10 mL
1 TSP. DRY MUSTARD	5 mL
DASH CAYENNE PEPPER	
½ - ¾ CUP BEER	125 - 175 mL
ROUND LOAF OF RYE, SOURDOUGH OR PUMPERNICKLE BREAD	

COMBINE ALL INGREDIENTS EXCEPT BREAD. SET
ASIDE. SLICE TOP OFF LOAF (BEST DONE WHEN SLIGHTLY
FROZEN). USING A SHARP KNIFE, SLICE AROUND RIM
LEAVING ½" SIDES. PULL OUT BREAD AND CUT INTO 1" CUBES.
PUT IN PLASTIC BAG UNTIL READY TO SERVE. FILL BREAD
WITH CHEESE MIXTURE, WRAP WITH FOIL AND BAKE AT
400° FOR 15 MINUTES OR UNTIL BUBBLY. PLACE ON A
PLATTER AND SERVE WITH BREAD CUBES AROUND LOAF.

ALL THIS SHAKING AND BAKING, THAWING, READY
MIXING, BOILING PLASTIC BAGS, OPENING CANS —
I TELL YOU, I'M SICK AND TIRED OF COOKING!

SMOKED OYSTER SPREAD

1 - 8 OZ. PKG. CREAM CHEESE - SOFTENED	250 g
1/4 CUP WHIPPING CREAM - WHIPPED	50 mL
1 TBSP. CHOPPED ONION	15 mL
1 TBSP. CHOPPED PARSLEY	15 mL
1 - 4 OZ. CAN SMOKED OYSTERS - DRAINED & CHOPPED	105 g
1 TSP. BRANDY	5 mL
1/4 TSP. WORCESTERSHIRE SAUCE	1 mL
DASH OF TABASCO	

MIX CREAM CHEESE WITH WHIPPING CREAM UNTIL SMOOTH. ADD THE ONION AND PARSLEY. MIX WELL. FOLD IN THE OYSTERS AND BRANDY. ADD WORCESTERSHIRE AND TABASCO. SERVE WITH ASSORTED CRACKERS.

MAKES ONE CUP.

LADY TO A HANDSOME MAN:
"YOU LOOK LIKE MY 3RD HUSBAND".
HIM: "HOW MANY HAVE YOU HAD?"
LADY: "JUST TWO"

BOMB SHELTER CROUSTADES

THESE TASTY MUSHROOM FILLED 'TARTS'
COME FROM THE WIFE OF THE ARCHITECT WHO
DESIGNED PIERRE TRUDEAU'S BOMBSHELTER!

CROUSTADES:

24 SLICES - VERY THIN SLICED WHITE BREAD	
(LOW CALORIE BREAD IS THE PERFECT SIZE)	
2 TBSPS. BUTTER	30 mL

MUSHROOM FILLING:

3 TBSPS. ONION - VERY FINELY CHOPPED	45 mL
½ LB. MUSHROOMS - VERY FINELY CHOPPED	250 g
4 TBSPS. BUTTER	60 mL
2 TBSPS. FLOUR	30 mL
1 CUP WHIPPING CREAM	250 mL
3 TBSPS. DRY WHITE WINE	45 mL
½ TSP. SALT	2 mL
PINCH - CAYENNE PEPPER	
1 TBSP. PARSLEY - FINELY CHOPPED	15 mL
1½ TBSPS. GREEN ONION - FINELY CHOPPED	22 mL
3 TBSPS. GRATED PARMESAN CHEESE	45 mL

CROUSTADES:

GENEROUSLY BUTTER SMALL MUFFIN TINS.
CUT A 3" ROUND FROM EACH SLICE OF BREAD.
CAREFULLY FIT THESE INTO THE MUFFIN TINS.

BOMB SHELTER CROUSTADES

THIS RECIPE CONTINUED FROM PAGE 48

BAKE THE CROUSTADES IN 400° OVEN FOR 10 MINUTES, OR UNTIL RIMS ARE LIGHTLY BROWNED. REMOVE FROM TINS AND COOL (MAY BE FROZEN AT THIS POINT).

FILLING:

IN A FRYING PAN, MELT BUTTER, ADD ONIONS AND MUSHROOMS. STIR AND COOK TILL ALL THE MOISTURE IS EVAPORATED. SPRINKLE WITH FLOUR. STIR THOROUGHLY. ADD CREAM, STIR CONSTANTLY UNTIL IT BOILS. ADD WINE, REDUCE HEAT AND SIMMER A FEW MINUTES LONGER. REMOVE FROM HEAT, STIR IN SALT, CAYENNE, PARSLEY AND GREEN ONION. TRANSFER TO A BOWL. COVER AND REFRIGERATE UNTIL NEEDED.

TO SERVE:

PREHEAT OVEN TO 350°. SPOON MUSHROOM FILLING INTO CROUSTADES; LIGHTLY SPRINKLE WITH PARMESAN AND PLACE ON COOKIE SHEET. HEAT IN OVEN 10 MINUTES — THEN BRIEFLY UNDER THE BROILER. SERVES 8 DELIGHTED GUESTS.

SORTA CURRIED, SORTA GLAZED, SORTA SWEET CHICKEN WINGS.

2 TBSPS. BUTTER	30 mL
½ CUP HONEY	125 mL
¼ CUP PREPARED MUSTARD	50 mL
½ – 1 TSP. CURRY POWDER (TO TASTE)	2–5 mL
1 DOZ. CHICKEN WINGS	XII
¼ CUP SESAME SEEDS	50 mL

COMBINE BUTTER, HONEY, MUSTARD, CURRY POWDER AND HEAT UNTIL BLENDED. BAKE CHICKEN WINGS ON COOKIE SHEET AT 400° (200°C) FOR 15 MINUTES. BASTE WITH SAUCE AND CONTINUE COOKING UNTIL BROWN, ABOUT 20 MINUTES. REMOVE FROM OVEN AND DIP IN SESAME SEEDS.

THE PERSON WHO IS BORED WHEN HE IS ALONE SHOULD UNDERSTAND THE POSITION OF OTHERS WHEN HE'S AROUND.

PICTURED ON OVERLEAF:

ARIZONA FRUIT SALAD- PAGE 86

SALMON PASTA SALAD - PAGE 82

PITA TOAST - PAGE 31

EASY SALMON PATÉ

1	7½ OZ. CAN RED SALMON - DRAINED	213 g
1	TBSP. ONION - MINCED	15 mL
1	TBSP. FRESH LEMON JUICE	15 mL
¼	TSP. LEMON RIND - GRATED	1 mL
2	TBSPS. MAYONNAISE	30 mL
½	CUP BUTTER OR MARGARINE - MELTED	125 mL
2	TSPS. FRESH DILL - SNIPPED OR...	10 mL
¼	TSP. DRIED DILL	1 mL
	SALT & PEPPER TO TASTE	

BLEND ALL INGREDIENTS TO SMOOTH CONSISTENCY. POUR INTO A CROCK OR SERVING BOWL. COVER AND CHILL SEVERAL HOURS OR OVERNIGHT. GARNISH WITH SPRIG OF DILL AND SERVE WITH MELBA TOAST OR ASSORTED CRACKERS. MAKES 1½ CUPS. FREEZES WELL.

" YOU MUST REMEMBER THIS
A KISS IS STILL A KISS
A HAT IS STILL A HAT "

CHEF TONER'S MUSSEL CREOLE

4	CUPS MUSSELS - TRIMMED, SCRAPED & WASHED*	1 L
¼	CUP WHITE WINE	50 mL
1	TBSP. SHALLOTS - FINELY CHOPPED OR	
	1 TBSP. GREEN ONIONS - FINELY CHOPPED	15 mL
1	TBSP. PARSLEY - CHOPPED	15 mL
¼	TSP. THYME	1 mL
¼	OF A BAY LEAF	
2	TBSPS. BUTTER	30 mL
¼	CUP TOMATO - PEELED & CHOPPED	50 mL
2	TBSPS. KETCHUP OR CHILI SAUCE	30 mL
½	TSP. TABASCO SAUCE	2 mL
½	TSP. WORCESTERSHIRE SAUCE	2 mL
1½	TBSPS. BUTTER	22 mL
	SALT & PEPPER TO TASTE	

(*NOTE: DISCARD ANY MUSSELS THAT ARE NOT TIGHTLY CLOSED - OR BETTER YET, TRY NOT TO BUY THEM.)

HEAT A LARGE HEAVY POT. WHEN VERY HOT, ADD MUSSELS AND WHITE WINE, COVER AND STEAM FOR 2 TO 3 MINUTES. ADD NEXT 9 INGREDIENTS AND COOK, COVERED, FOR 2 MINUTES OR UNTIL SHELLS OPEN. REMOVE MUSSELS TO SERVING PLATE AND KEEP WARM. CONTINUE COOKING SAUCE ON HIGH FOR ONE MINUTE. ADD BUTTER. SEASON WITH SALT AND PEPPER. POUR SAUCE OVER MUSSELS AND SERVE IMMEDIATELY.

HOT 'N' SPICY WINGS

GET OUT THE FINGER BOWLS FOR EVERYONE'S FAVOURITE.

3 LBS. CHICKEN WINGS	1.5 kg.
½ CUP KETCHUP	125 mL
¼ CUP WATER	50 mL
¼ CUP HONEY	50 mL
¼ CUP RED WINE VINEGAR	50 mL
2 TBSPS. BROWN SUGAR, PACKED	30 mL
1 TBSP. DIJON MUSTARD	15 mL
1 TBSP. WORCESTERSHIRE SAUCE	15 mL
1 TBSP. SOYA SAUCE	15 mL
2 TBSPS. HOT PEPPER SAUCE	30 mL
2 CLOVES GARLIC - MINCED	
2 TBSPS. DRY MINCED ONIONS	30 mL

REMOVE TIPS FROM WINGS. COVER A BROILER PAN WITH FOIL. POKE HOLES IN FOIL. ARRANGE WINGS IN SINGLE LAYER. PLACE UNDER BROILER UNTIL LIGHTLY BROWNED. IN A SAUCE PAN, MIX ALL INGREDIENTS AND BRING TO A BOIL; REDUCE HEAT AND SIMMER FOR 5 TO 10 MINUTES. USING TONGS, DIP EACH WING IN HOT SAUCE AND PLACE ON BAKING SHEET THEN BAKE AT 375° FOR 35 TO 40 MINUTES. BASTE WITH REMAINING SAUCE DURING BAKING. DURING THE LAST FEW MINUTES, TURN ON BROILER AND CRISP WINGS.

CHIPPY KNEES BITES

GAME MISCONDUCT IF YOU DON'T TRY THEM!

1 - 4 OZ. CAN CHOPPED, MILD GREEN CHILIES 115 mL
4 CUPS GRATED SHARP CHEDDAR CHEESE 1 L
6 EGGS
1 TBSP. FINELY CHOPPED ONION   15 mL

GREASE AN 8" x 8" (20 x 20 cm) BAKING PAN. SPREAD CHILIES EVENLY OVER BOTTOM, SPRINKLE GRATED CHEESE OVER CHILIES. BEAT EGGS AND ADD ONION. POUR OVER CHEESE. BAKE AT 350° FOR 30 MINUTES (OR UNTIL EGGS ARE FIRM). CUT INTO 1" SQUARES.

DILLED OYSTER CRACKERS

A GREAT LITTLE APPETIZER!

4 CUPS (11 OZ.) OYSTER CRACKERS   312 g
1 OZ. PKG. HIDDEN VALLEY RANCH STYLE
         DRESSING MIX   28 g
1 TBSP. DILL WEED   15 mL
3/4 CUP SALAD OIL   175 mL
1 TSP. GARLIC POWDER   5 mL

COMBINE ALL INGREDIENTS IN A PLASTIC COVERED CONTAINER. SHAKE OFTEN. LET STAND OVERNIGHT, OR AT LEAST 6 HOURS.

BRANDY-NUT BRIE

WHAT COULD BE EASIER??

1/4 CUP BROWN SUGAR - PACKED	50 mL
1/4 CUP PECANS OR CASHEWS - CHOPPED	50 mL
1 TBSP. BRANDY OR WHISKEY	15 mL
1 - 4" ROUND BRIE CHEESE	235 g
CRACKERS	

GET READY.... STIR TOGETHER SUGAR, NUTS AND BRANDY. PLACE CHEESE ON AN OVEN PROOF PLATTER AND BAKE AT 500° FOR 4 TO 5 MINUTES UNTIL CHEESE IS SOFTENED. MOUND SUGAR MIXTURE OVER TOP. BAKE 2 TO 3 MINUTES MORE UNTIL SUGAR IS MELTED.

FOR MICROWAVE: PLACE SUGAR MIXTURE IN GLASS MEASURING CUP AND COOK UNCOVERED FOR 1 MINUTE ON HIGH OR UNTIL SUGAR IS MELTED. PLACE CHEESE ON MICROWAVE SAFE PLATE, POUR SUGAR MIXTURE OVER AND COOK UNCOVERED ON MEDIUM ABOUT 2 MINUTES. CHEESE SHOULD BE HEATED THROUGH BUT NOT MELTED.

WHEN YOUR KIDS ARE FIT TO LIVE WITH,
THEY'RE LIVING WITH SOMEONE ELSE.

SPANAKOPITA

A SHORT-CUT ROUTE TO GREEK GOURMET.

2	BUNCHES SPINACH	
1⅓	CUP ONION - DICED	325 mL
½	CUP MUSHROOMS - DICED	125 mL
	SALT & PEPPER TO TASTE	
2	EGGS - BEATEN	
½	LB. FETA CHEESE - CRUMBLED	250 g
⅓	CUP BREAD CRUMBS	75 mL
1	TSP. DRIED DILL	5 mL
	HEALTHY PINCH NUTMEG	
	SALT & PEPPER TO TASTE	
¼	LB. BUTTER - MELTED	125 mL
12	SHEETS PHYLLO DOUGH	

WASH, STEM AND STEAM SPINACH UNTIL WILTED; CHOP. SAUTÉ ONIONS, MUSHROOMS, SALT AND PEPPER UNTIL LIQUID HAS EVAPORATED (ABOUT 5 MINUTES). ADD TO SPINACH. ADD EGGS, CHEESE, BREAD CRUMBS, DILL AND SPICES. FOLLOW PACKAGE INSTRUCTIONS FOR KEEPING PHYLLO MOIST. BRUSH EACH SHEET WITH BUTTER, LAYERING 4 SHEETS ON TOP OF EACH OTHER. PUT FILLING ALONG LENGTH OF TOP LAYER, LEAVING 1" MARGIN AT EACH EDGE. SEAL BY FOLDING AND ROLLING UP LIKE A JELLY ROLL. BRUSH TOPS WITH BUTTER AND BAKE AT 425° FOR 20 MINUTES. COOL 10 MINUTES. SLICE AND SERVE. MESSY BUT MARVELLOUS! MAY BE REHEATED IN MICROWAVE.
MAKES 3 ROLLS.

ASPARAGUS CHICKEN PUFFS

1	LARGE CHICKEN BREAST - FILLETED & COOKED	
2	TBSPS. MAYONNAISE	30 mL
½ TO 1 TSP.	CURRY POWDER	2-5 mL
	SALT & PEPPER TO TASTE	
1 - 14 OZ. PKG.	PUFF PASTRY	397 g
1 - 12 OZ. CAN	ASPARAGUS - WELL DRAINED	341 mL
1	EGG - BEATEN	
	SESAME SEEDS	

IN A FOOD PROCESSOR, BLEND CHICKEN, MAYONNAISE, CURRY, SALT AND PEPPER UNTIL SMOOTH. ROLL PASTRY INTO RECTANGULAR SHAPE, 10" x 14". CUT LENGTHWISE INTO 3 EVEN STRIPS. SPREAD CHICKEN MIXTURE ALONG ONE SIDE OF EACH STRIP OF PASTRY. PLACE ASPARAGUS SPEARS LENGTHWISE BESIDE CHICKEN MIXTURE. BRUSH EDGES OF PASTRY WITH EGG. ROLL PASTRY OVER TO CLOSE COMPLETELY. BRUSH TOP WITH EGG, CUT ROLLS DIAGONALLY INTO 1" PIECES AND SPRINKLE WITH SESAME SEEDS. PLACE ON GREASED COOKIE SHEET AND BAKE AT 450° FOR 10 MINUTES. LOWER OVEN TO 350° FOR ANOTHER 10 MINUTES OR UNTIL GOLDEN BROWN. MAKES 48 PUFFS; (LIKE SMOKE SIGNAL: "GOOD").

A CHILD IS A PERSON WHO CAN'T UNDERSTAND WHY SOMEONE WOULD GIVE AWAY A PERFECTLY GOOD CAT.

AUNTY LIL'S SIMPLE ANTIPASTO

1 – 12 oz. BOTTLE HOT KETCHUP	375 mL
1 – 10 oz. BOTTLE CHILI SAUCE	284 mL
1 – 4 oz. JAR PIMENTO OLIVE PIECES	SMALL JAR
1 – 12 oz. JAR SWEET GREEN RELISH	375 mL
1 – 10 oz. CAN MUSHROOMS – DRAINED	284 mL
2 – 7 oz. CANS CRAB OR SHRIMP – DRAINED	396 mL
1 – 7 oz. CAN SOLID WHITE TUNA – BROKEN	198 mL
TABASCO SAUCE TO TASTE	

MIX ALL INGREDIENTS IN LARGE SAUCE PAN. BRING TO BOIL AND SIMMER FOR 5 MINUTES. FILL AND SEAL IN STERILIZED JARS. PLACE ON RACK IN CANNER AND ADD 3" WATER. BRING TO BOIL AND SIMMER FOR 20 MINUTES. THEN, KEEP IT COOL.

MOST OF US CAN FORGIVE AND FORGET – WE JUST DON'T WANT THE OTHER PERSON TO FORGET WHAT WE FORGAVE!

3	TBSPS. BUTTER	45 mL
1	TBSP. SESAME OIL	15 mL
1	TSP. CAYENNE PEPPER	5 mL
½	CUP DIJON MUSTARD	125 mL
⅓	CUP CIDER VINEGAR	75 mL
2	TBSPS. BROWN SUGAR-FIRMLY PACKED	30 mL
3	TBSPS. HONEY	45 mL
1	TBSP. SOYA SAUCE	15 mL
2	LBS. CHICKEN BREAST - SKINNED, BONED & CUT INTO 1" CUBES	1 kg

MELT THE BUTTER AND OIL IN A PAN, ADD THE REMAINING INGREDIENTS, EXCEPT THE CHICKEN AND SIMMER FOR 5 MINUTES. ADD THE CHICKEN AND SAUTÉ UNTIL THE CHICKEN IS BROWNED ON ALL SIDES. SERVE THE CHICKEN WITH THE SAUCE IN A CHAFING DISH WITH TOOTHPICKS. GARNISH WITH PARSLEY.

SHE'S A LIGHT EATER - AS SOON AS IT'S LIGHT SHE STARTS EATING!

A LIGHT, ELEGANT APPETIZER SERVED IN A CHAFING DISH.

1	LB. ASSORTED COOKED SEAFOOD:	
	SHRIMP, LOBSTER, SCALLOPS	500 g
½	CUP DRY WHITE WINE	125 mL
¼	CUP OIL	50 mL
2	TSPS. MINCED ONION	10 mL
¼	TSP. CRUSHED ROSEMARY	1 mL
2	TBSPS. BUTTER	30 mL
1	TBSP. LEMON JUICE	15 mL

COOK SEAFOOD ACCORDING TO PACKAGE DIRECTIONS AND CUT INTO BITE-SIZED PIECES. LEAVE SCALLOPS WHOLE. COMBINE WINE, OIL, ONION AND ROSEMARY AND MARINATE SEAFOOD IN FRIDGE FOR SEVERAL HOURS. DRAIN AND RESERVE LIQUID. PLACE SEAFOOD IN CHAFING DISH. MELT BUTTER, ADD LEMON JUICE AND MARINADE. POUR OVER SEAFOOD. HEAT AND SERVE WARM WITH COCKTAIL PICKS.

SOME CHILDREN ARE LIKE POLITICIANS; YOU SEE THEM ONLY WHEN THEY NEED HELP.

COCKTAIL SPREAD

GUESTS WILL ASK FOR A SPOON! JIMMY DID!

8 oz. CREAM CHEESE		250 mL
½ CUP SOUR CREAM		125 mL
¼ CUP MAYONNAISE		50 mL
3 - 4 oz. TINS BROKEN SHRIMP - RINSED & DRAINED		3 - 125 mL
1 CUP SEAFOOD COCKTAIL SAUCE		250 mL
2 CUPS MOZZARELLA CHEESE - GRATED		500 mL
3 GREEN ONIONS - CHOPPED		
1 TOMATO - DICED		
1 GREEN PEPPER - CHOPPED		

MIX FIRST 3 INGREDIENTS TOGETHER. SPREAD IN A 12" DISH OR PIE PLATE. SCATTER SHRIMP OVER CHEESE MIXTURE. ADD LAYER OF SEAFOOD SAUCE, THEN MOZZARELLA CHEESE, GREEN ONIONS, TOMATO AND GREEN PEPPER. COVER UNTIL READY TO SERVE. SERVE WITH CRACKERS.

SOME PEOPLE HAVE LOUSY MEMORIES —
THEY NEVER FORGET ANYTHING!

HAM AND CHEESE PUFFS

THEY FREEZE WELL. IF YOU'VE GOT TENNIS ELBOW—YOU'LL NEED HELP BEATING THESE.

1	CUP WATER	250 mL
1/3	CUP BUTTER	75 mL
1	CUP FLOUR	250 mL
4	EGGS	
1 1/2	CUPS SHARP CHEDDAR CHEESE - GRATED	375 mL
1	CUP HAM OR CRISP BACON - FINELY CHOPPED	250 mL
1/2 TO 1	TSP. DRY MUSTARD	2-5 mL
1 - 4 OZ.	CAN CHOPPED JALAPEÑOS - DRAINED	114 mL
	- (OPTIONAL)	

COMBINE WATER AND BUTTER IN A HEAVY SAUCEPAN AND BRING TO A BOIL. REMOVE FROM HEAT AND ADD FLOUR ALL AT ONCE. BEAT WITH A WOODEN SPOON UNTIL WELL - MIXED. RETURN TO MEDIUM HEAT AND BEAT UNTIL MIXTURE LEAVES SIDES OF PAN & FORMS A BALL. REMOVE FROM HEAT AND BEAT IN EGGS ONE AT A TIME TO FORM A SMOOTH MIXTURE (BE PATIENT AND BEAT THOROUGLY). STIR IN CHEESE, HAM, MUSTARD AND JALAPEÑOS (IF DESIRED). DROP BY SMALL TEASPOONFULS ONTO GREASED COOKIE SHEET. BAKE AT 400° FOR 15 TO 20 MINUTES. REHEAT IF FROZEN IN 350° FOR 5 TO 10 MINUTES.

JOIN THE FUTURE NOW BEFORE IT'S SOLD OUT.

TART SHELLS:

36 SLICES VERY THIN SLICED WHITE BREAD
(LOW CALORIE BREAD IS THE PERFECT SIZE).

3 TBSPS. BUTTER   45 mL

CRAB FILLING:

3 TBSPS. BUTTER	45 mL
1/4 CUP FLOUR	50 mL
1 1/2 CUPS. MILK	375 mL
1 CUP CHEDDAR CHEESE - GRATED	250 mL
1 - 7 1/2 oz. CAN CRABMEAT	198 g
1 TBSP. GREEN ONION - MINCED	15 mL
1 TSP. LEMON RIND - GRATED	5 mL
1 TBSP. LEMON JUICE	15 mL
2 TBSPS. PARSLEY	30 mL
1 TSP. WORCESTERSHIRE SAUCE	5 mL
1 TSP. PREPARED MUSTARD	5 mL
1/2 TSP. SALT	2 mL

DASH OF TABASCO

TART SHELLS: GENEROUSLY BUTTER SMALL MUFFIN TINS. CUT A 3" ROUND FROM EACH SLICE OF BREAD. PRESS INTO MUFFIN TINS. BAKE AT 400° FOR 10 MINUTES OR UNTIL GOLDEN. FILLING: MELT 3 TBSPS. BUTTER, STIR IN FLOUR, COOK UNTIL BUBBLY. STIR IN MILK; COOK, STIRRING UNTIL THICKENED. STIR IN CHEESE UNTIL MELTED. ADD REMAINING INGREDIENTS. FILL EACH TARTLET WITH MIXTURE. BAKE AT 400° FOR 5 MINUTES OR UNTIL BUBBLY. MAKES 3 DOZEN - FREEZES WELL.

MULLIGATAWNY SOUP

A BRITISH - INDIAN SOUP - POPULAR WITH THE RANKS - GUNGA DIN LOVED IT!

2	TBSPS. BUTTER	30 mL
3	STALKS, CELERY - SLICED	
1	LARGE POTATO - PEELED AND DICED	
2	LARGE ONIONS - CHOPPED FINELY	
4	CLOVES GARLIC - CHOPPED FINELY	
2	CARROTS - DICED	
4	TSPS. CURRY POWDER	20 mL
1/4	TSP. GROUND CLOVES	1 mL
1/2	TSP. GROUND GINGER	2 mL
2	TSPS. CAYENNE	10 mL
1 TO 2	TSPS. SALT	5 - 10 mL
2	TSPS. PEPPER	10 mL
8	CUPS CHICKEN OR TURKEY BROTH	2 L
3	CUPS DICED CHICKEN OR TURKEY, COOKED	750 mL
3	CUPS COOKED RICE	750 mL
2	GRANNY SMITH APPLES - PEELED AND GRATED	
2	TBSPS. LEMON JUICE	30 mL
1	CUP PLAIN YOGURT	250 mL

IN A LARGE POT MELT BUTTER AND SAUTÉ CELERY, POTATO, ONION, GARLIC, CARROT AND SEASONINGS FOR 5 MINUTES. ADD BROTH AND SIMMER 20 MINUTES. ADD CHICKEN / TURKEY, RICE, APPLES AND LEMON JUICE. BEFORE SERVING ADD YOGURT AND HEAT TO NEAR BOILING. 18 LADLES WORTH.

AVGOLÉMONO SOUP

WELL, THE GREEKS CAN SAY IT!
(THEY ALSO SAY: "IT'S GOOD")

6 CUPS	CHICKEN OR TURKEY BROTH	1.5 L
1/4 CUP	LONG GRAIN RICE	50 mL
1 TSP.	SALT	5 mL
3	EGGS	
1/4 CUP	FRESH LEMON JUICE	50 mL
1	LEMON, SLICED THINLY	

COMBINE BROTH, RICE AND SALT IN LARGE POT AND BRING TO BOIL. COVER AND SIMMER UNTIL RICE IS TENDER (ABOUT 25 MINUTES). COOL ONLY SLIGHTLY. BEAT THE EGGS IN A BOWL UNTIL THICK, THEN BEAT IN LEMON JUICE. CAREFULLY STIR 2 CUPS OF BROTH INTO EGG MIXTURE AND BEAT WELL. RETURN TO SOUP POT AND BEAT UNTIL SLIGHTLY THICKENED. COOL AND REFRIGERATE. SOUP WILL THICKEN AS IT BECOMES WELL CHILLED. STIR BEFORE SERVING. GARNISH WITH LEMON SLICES. SERVES 6.

THE THREE WISEMEN - TAX ACCOUNTANT, LAWYER AND GOLF PRO.

AVOCADO SOUP

A RICH, ELEGANT STARTER!

2 LARGE AVOCADOS - PEELED & HALVED	
1 CUP WHIPPING CREAM	250 mL
½ CUP MILK	125 mL
1 - 10 oz. CAN CHICKEN BROTH	284 mL
1 TO 2 TSPS. LIME JUICE	5 - 10 mL
1 TSP. 'MAGGI' SEASONING	5 mL
1 TSP. WHITE PEPPER	5 mL
SALT TO TASTE	
SOUR CREAM OR CRISP BACON - CRUMBLED	
FRESH CHIVES - CHOPPED	

PLACE AVOCADO IN BLENDER. ADD WHIPPING CREAM, MILK, BROTH, LIME JUICE, 'MAGGI' SEASONING, PEPPER AND SALT. BLEND UNTIL SMOOTH. CHILL. WHEN READY TO SERVE, ADD A SPOONFUL OF SOUR CREAM OR BACON AND GARNISH WITH CHIVES. SERVES 4 TO 6. SERVE CHILLED.

YOU HAVE TWO CHOICES FOR DINNER —
TAKE IT OR LEAVE IT!

PICTURED ON OVERLEAF:

PASTA WITH CRAB AND BASIL- PAGE 134

CREAM OF PARSLEY AND BASIL SOUP

A LIGHT, REFRESHING STARTER.

3	TBSPS. BUTTER	45 mL
1½	CUPS FRESH PARSLEY	375 mL
½	CUP FRESH BASIL - STEMS REMOVED	125 mL
2	CUPS CHICKEN STOCK	500 mL
3	MEDIUM POTATOES - PEELED & CUT INTO CHUNKS	
3	CUPS LIGHT CREAM	750 mL
	SALT, PEPPER & NUTMEG TO TASTE	

HEAT BUTTER IN LARGE SAUCEPAN OVER LOW HEAT. ADD PARSLEY AND BASIL. SIMMER FOR 5 MINUTES; ADD STOCK AND POTATOES, COVER AND SIMMER 20 MINUTES. COOL SLIGHTLY, ADD CREAM AND BLEND UNTIL SMOOTH. ADD SEASONINGS. SERVE HOT. GARNISH WITH BASIL LEAF. SERVES 4 TO 6.

SMILE! IT'S THE SECOND BEST THING YOU CAN DO WITH YOUR LIPS.

CREAM OF SPINACH SOUP

POPEYE NEVER HAD IT SO GOOD; EVEN WITHOUT OLIVE OIL! THIS WILL SERVE 4.

2 CUPS CHICKEN BROTH		500 mL
1 PKG. - 10 OZ. FROZEN CHOPPED SPINACH		300 g
¾ CUP WHIPPING CREAM		175 mL
SALT AND PEPPER TO TASTE		
2 SLICES BACON, COOKED CRISP AND CRUMBLED; —OPTIONAL		

SIMMER CHICKEN BROTH AND FROZEN SPINACH UNTIL SPINACH IS COMPLETELY THAWED. PURÉE MIXTURE IN BLENDER OR FOOD PROCESSOR. RETURN TO SAUCEPAN AND STIR IN CREAM AND SALT AND PEPPER. ADD BACON IF DESIRED. SIMMER ABOUT 5 MINUTES OR UNTIL PIPING HOT.

TO ERR IS HUMAN, BUT TO BLAME IT ON SOMEONE ELSE IS HUMANER.

CAULIFLOWER SOUP WITH BLEU CHEESE

2 - 10 OZ. PKGS. CHOPPED FROZEN CAULIFLOWER	2-283 g
OR 4 CUPS FRESH CAULIFLOWER	1 L
1/4 CUP ONION - FINELY CHOPPED	50 mL
2 CUPS CHICKEN BROTH	500 mL
2 OZ. BLEU CHEESE	55 g
2 TBSPS. BUTTER	30 mL
1 TBSP. FLOUR	15 mL
1 TSP. SALT	5 mL
PEPPER TO TASTE	
PINCH OF MACE OR NUTMEG	
2 CUPS HALF AND HALF CREAM	500 mL

THAW CAULIFLOWER AND COMBINE WITH ONION AND BROTH. BRING TO A BOIL, REDUCE HEAT AND SIMMER 10 MINUTES. ADD CHEESE AND BLENDERIZE TO A SMOOTH CONSISTENCY. IN A LARGE SAUCEPAN, MELT BUTTER, ADD FLOUR, SALT, PEPPER AND MACE. SLOWLY ADD CREAM AND STIR UNTIL SMOOTH. ADD CAULIFLOWER MIXTURE. HEAT BEFORE SERVING. SERVES 6.

THE PERSON WHO COINED - "OUT OF SIGHT-OUT OF MIND" HAD NO CHILDREN OF DATING AGE OUT ON SATURDAY NIGHT!

POTATO SOUP

THE SOUR CREAM MAKES THE DIFFERENCE.

4 LARGE POTATOES – PEELED & DICED	
½ CUP CELERY - DICED	125 mL
½ CUP ONION - DICED	125 mL
1½ CUPS WATER	375 mL
4 CHICKEN BOUILLON CUBES	
½ TSP. SALT	2 mL
2 CUPS MILK	500 mL
2 CUPS SOUR CREAM	500 mL
1 TBSP. FLOUR	15 mL
PARSLEY OR GREEN ONIONS (FOR GARNISH)	

PUT POTATOES, CELERY, ONION, WATER, BOUILLON CUBES AND SALT IN LARGE POT. COVER AND COOK UNTIL VEGETABLES ARE TENDER – APPROXIMATELY 20 MINUTES. REMOVE FROM STOVE AND MIX WITH ELECTRIC MIXER UNTIL MIXTURE IS A SMOOTH PASTE. ADD 1 CUP MILK AND HEAT. IN MEDIUM BOWL, BLEND SOUR CREAM WITH FLOUR. STIR IN 1 CUP MILK. VERY SLOWLY, POUR ⅓ OF THE HEATED MIXTURE INTO SOUR CREAM. POUR THIS MIXTURE SLOWLY INTO THE REMAINDER OF SOUP MIXTURE. HEAT AND STIR UNTIL THICKENED. SERVES 6.

MUSHROOM AND LEEK SOUP

A WINTER TREAT FOR YOUR DINNER GUESTS—
OR YOUR FAMILY! MAKES 6 SMALL SERVINGS.

2 BUNCHES LEEKS, WASHED WELL (TO REMOVE ANY SAND)
1/4 CUP BUTTER   50 mL
1/2 LB. MUSHROOMS – FINELY CHOPPED   250 g
1/4 CUP FLOUR   50 mL
1/2 TSP. SALT   2 mL
2 DASHES CAYENNE PEPPER
1 CUP CHICKEN BROTH
        (CHICKEN IN A MUG MIX IS FINE)   250 mL
3 TO 4 CUPS MILK   750 mL – 1 L
2 TBSPS. SHERRY OR 1 TBSP. LEMON JUICE   30 mL
6 LEMON SLICES
        FRESH PARSLEY

WASH AND FINELY CHOP WHITE PART OF LEEKS.
IN A HEAVY SAUCEPAN OVER MEDIUM HEAT, MELT
BUTTER AND SAUTÉ LEEKS UNTIL TENDER, BUT
NOT BROWN. REMOVE FROM PAN AND SET ASIDE.
IN REMAINING BUTTER, SAUTÉ CHOPPED MUSHROOMS
TILL SOFT – ABOUT 5 MINUTES. (DON'T WORRY ABOUT
EXTRA JUICE.) BLEND IN FLOUR, SALT AND CAYENNE
PEPPER. ADD LEEKS. GRADUALLY STIR IN CHICKEN
BROTH, MILK AND SHERRY (OR LEMON JUICE). COOK
UNTIL THICKENED AND MIXTURE COMES TO A BOIL.
SIMMER 10 MINUTES. SERVE WITH THIN SLICES
OF LEMON AND A SPRINKLE OF PARSLEY.

KILLER COLE SLAW

ANOTHER FOREVER FAMILY FAVOURITE!

SALAD INGREDIENTS:

½ CABBAGE - CHOPPED
5 STALKS ·GREEN ONIONS - CHOPPED
¼ CUP SLIVERED ALMONDS — TOASTED   50 mL
¼ CUP SUNFLOWER SEEDS — TOASTED   50 mL
     (OR SESAME SEEDS)
1 PKG. JAPANESE NOODLE SOUP MIX—
     CRUSHED UP (ICHIBAN)
(-SAVE SEASONING PACKAGE FOR DRESSING)

DRESSING:

¼ CUP RICE (OR WHITE) VINEGAR   50 mL
¼ CUP SALAD OIL   50 mL
    SEASONING PACKAGE FROM NOODLES

COMBINE ALL SALAD INGREDIENTS EXCEPT NOODLES. BEFORE SERVING, TOSS WITH THE DRESSING. ADD CRUNCHED UP NOODLES AND TOSS AGAIN. SERVES 6. IF THERE'S ANY LEFT OVER— SAVE IT! KIDS LOVE IT THE NEXT DAY!

CAN YOU IMAGINE THE INCREDIBLE COURAGE IT TOOK TO FIRST DISCOVER FROGS LEGS WERE EDIBLE?

ZUCCHINI SALAD

GREAT FIRST COURSE OR USE DRESSING AS A DIP!

1	CUP MAYONNAISE	250 mL
½	CUP SOUR CREAM	125 mL
½	CUP PARSLEY - CHOPPED	125 mL
3	GREEN ONIONS - CHOPPED	
3	TBSPS. WHITE WINE VINEGAR	45 mL
½	TSP. DRIED TARRAGON LEAVES	2 mL
1	TSP. WORCESTERSHIRE SAUCE	5 mL
½	TSP. DRY MUSTARD	2 mL
¼	TSP. BLACK PEPPER - FRESHLY GROUND	1 mL
2	CLOVES GARLIC	
1	TBSP. FRESH LEMON JUICE	15 mL
2	TBSPS. CHIVES - CHOPPED	30 mL
8	MEDIUM ZUCCHINI - THINLY SLICED ON DIAGONAL	
	CHERRY TOMATOES FOR GARNISH	

PLACE ALL INGREDIENTS EXCEPT ZUCCHINI AND CHERRY TOMATOES IN A BLENDER OR FOOD PROCESSOR AND BLEND THOROUGHLY. TOSS ZUCCHINI WITH DRESSING. MOUND ON CRISP LETTUCE LEAVES AND GARNISH WITH CHERRY TOMATOES. SERVES 6.

NEVER INSULT AN ALLIGATOR UNTIL YOU'VE CROSSED THE RIVER.

RUSSIAN BEET SALAD

GREAT FOR A BUFFET - WHY NOT RUSH IN TO IT!

1 16 oz. CAN BEETS - SLICED	500 mL
1 3¾ oz. PKG. LEMON JELLO	85 g
¼ CUP SUGAR	50 mL
¼ CUP VINEGAR	50 mL
1 TBSP. PREPARED HORSERADISH	15 mL
2 TSPS. LEMON JUICE	10 mL
1 - 4 oz. PKG. CREAM CHEESE	125 g
MILK OR CREAM	
1 TBSP. MAYONNAISE	15 mL

DRAIN BEETS, RESERVING LIQUID AND SLICE INTO SHOESTRINGS. ADD ENOUGH WATER TO BEET JUICE TO MAKE 1½ CUPS. BRING LIQUID TO A BOIL. ADD JELLO AND STIR UNTIL JELLO IS DISSOLVED. COOL AND ADD SUGAR, VINEGAR, HORSERADISH AND LEMON JUICE. ADD BEETS AND POUR INTO A 9" x 9" GLASS DISH AND REFRIGERATE UNTIL SALAD IS COMPLETELY SET. MIX CREAM CHEESE AND MAYONNAISE ADDING ENOUGH MILK UNTIL IT IS THE CONSISTENCY OF ICING. SPREAD OVER TOP OF SALAD AND REFRIGERATE UNTIL SERVING TIME.

A DIAMOND IS A CHUNK OF COAL THAT MADE
GOOD UNDER PRESSURE!

A DIFFERENT SPINACH SALAD

THE DRESSING REALLY HAS ADDED ZIP!

1	PKG. FRESH SPINACH	
1	HEAD BUTTER LETTUCE	
2	CUPS FRESH BEAN SPROUTS	500 mL
1	CAN WATER CHESTNUTS (DRAINED & SLICED)	
¾	CUP BACON-COOKED & CRUMBLED	175 mL

DRESSING:

½	CUP SALAD OIL	125 mL
¼	CUP SUGAR	50 mL
¼	CUP KETCHUP	50 mL
2	TBSPS. RED WINE VINEGAR	30 mL
½	TSP. WORCESTERSHIRE SAUCE	2 mL
1	SMALL ONION-FINELY CHOPPED	
¼	TSP. DRY MUSTARD	1 mL
½	TSP. SALT	2 mL
¼ TO ½	TSP. CAYENNE PEPPER	1-2 mL

WASH SPINACH AND LETTUCE, DRAIN AND DRY. COMBINE DRESSING INGREDIENTS AND BLEND 'TIL SMOOTH. SET IN FRIDGE FOR AT LEAST 1 HOUR. ADD DRESSING JUST BEFORE SERVING.

POVERTY: A STATE OF MIND BROUGHT ON BY A NEIGHBOUR'S NEW CAR.

ROMAINE WITH ORANGES AND PECANS

2 HEADS ROMAINE LETTUCE	
(WASH AND TEAR INTO BITE-SIZE PIECES)	
¾ TO 1 CUP PECAN HALVES - TOASTED	175 mL
2 ORANGES - PEELED & SLICED	
¼ CUP VINEGAR	50 mL
½ CUP SUGAR	125 mL
1 CUP VEGETABLE OIL	250 mL
1 TSP. SALT	5 mL
½ SMALL RED ONION - CHOPPED	
1 TSP. DRY MUSTARD	5 mL
2 TBSPS. WATER	30 mL

PLACE LETTUCE, ORANGES AND PECANS IN SALAD BOWL. COMBINE VINEGAR, OIL, SUGAR, SALT, ONION, MUSTARD AND WATER IN BLENDER. BLEND UNTIL WELL MIXED. MAKE AHEAD AND REFRIGERATE UNTIL READY TO TOSS SALAD.

DON'T USE ALL THE DRESSING! - SET ASIDE AND USE AS A DIP FOR FRESH FRUIT!

A HORSE, DIVIDED AGAINST ITSELF,
CANNOT STAND.

PAPAYA WITH SHRIMP
AND CURRY MAYONNAISE

THIS MAKES AN ELEGANT STARTER FOR A
SPECIAL DINNER OR CAN BE USED AS A
LUNCHEON SALAD.

1 CUP MAYONNAISE	250 mL
1/4 TSP. GINGER	1 mL
1/2 TO 1 TSP. CURRY POWDER	2-5 mL
1 TBSP. LIME JUICE	15 mL
1 TSP. HONEY	5 mL

COMBINE ALL INGREDIENTS AND WHISK UNTIL
SMOOTH. CHILL.

2 RIPE PAPAYAS	
1 HEAD BUTTER LETTUCE	
1 1/2 LBS. FRESH, COOKED SHRIMP	750 mL

PEEL AND SLICE PAPAYA, AND ARRANGE ON
LETTUCE WITH SHRIMP. TOP WITH CURRY
MAYONNAISE. MAKES 6 SALADS.

I'M MAKING MY FAVOURITE THING FOR DINNER—
RESERVATIONS.

SALMON PASTA SALAD

¾ TO 1 LB. FRESH SALMON FILLETS	375 - 500 g
⅛ TSP. SALT	.5 mL
1 TBSP. LEMON JUICE	15 mL
1 8 OZ. PKG. SPIRAL OR SHELL SHAPED PASTA,	
COOKED & DRAINED	250 g
ROMAINE LETTUCE LEAVES	
CUCUMBER SLICES	
DILL SPRIGS	

CUCUMBER DRESSING:

1 ENGLISH CUCUMBER	
¾ CUP SOUR CREAM	175 mL
¼ CUP MAYONNAISE	50 mL
2 TBSPS. FRESH DILL - CHOPPED	30 mL
1 TBSP. WHITE VINEGAR	15 mL
2 TBSPS. GREEN ONIONS - CHOPPED	30 mL
SALT & PEPPER, TO TASTE	

PLACE SALMON FILLETS, SKIN SIDE DOWN, IN SMALL BAKING PAN. SPRINKLE WITH SALT AND LEMON JUICE AND COVER WITH BUTTERED WAX PAPER, BUTTERED SIDE DOWN. BAKE IN PREHEATED 350° OVEN FOR 12 TO 15 MINUTES, OR UNTIL SALMON FLAKES EASILY. COOL AND REFRIGERATE, COVERED, UNTIL WELL CHILLED, ABOUT 2 HOURS.

THIS RECIPE CONTINUED NEXT PAGE.

SALMON PASTA SALAD

THIS RECIPE CONTINUED FROM 82.

TO PREPARE CUCUMBER DRESSING:

GRATE CUCUMBER, PLACE IN SIEVE AND LET DRAIN AT ROOM TEMPERATURE FOR AT LEAST ½ HOUR. COMBINE SOUR CREAM, MAYONNAISE, VINEGAR, DILL, GREEN ONION, SALT AND PEPPER IN SMALL BOWL. ADD THE GRATED CUCUMBER.

TO SERVE:

PUT PASTA IN BOWL AND TOSS WITH DRESSING. BREAK SALMON INTO PIECES AND GENTLY FOLD INTO SALAD. ARRANGE ON LETTUCE LEAVES AND GARNISH WITH CUCUMBER SLICES AND DILL SPRIGS. SERVES 8. SEE PICTURE, PAGE 51.

FRESH FRUIT DRESSING

LOW CAL-TASTES GREAT RIGHT OUT OF THE JAR!

⅔ CUP PLAIN YOGURT	150 mL
¼ CUP VEGETABLE OIL	50 mL
2 TBSPS. FROZEN ORANGE JUICE CONCENTRATE	30 mL
2 TBSPS. HONEY	30 mL
½ TSP. GRATED ORANGE RIND	2 mL

COMBINE ALL INGREDIENTS AND MIX WELL. REFRIGERATE IN A SEALED CONTAINER. MAKES ABOUT 1¼ C.

ASPARAGUS PASTA SALAD

A TASTY AND ATTRACTIVE LUNCHEON DISH,
SPRINGTIME PICNIC OR BUFFET!

2	CUPS SMALL PASTA SHELLS	500 mL
1	LB. ASPARAGUS—CUT INTO 2" PIECES, TOUGH ENDS DISCARDED	500 g
1	MEDIUM RED BELL PEPPER—CHOPPED	
1	CUP FRESH MUSHROOMS—SLICED	250 mL
1	CUP GREEN ONION—FINELY SLICED	250 mL
¼	CUP PARSLEY—FINELY CHOPPED	50 mL
2	TBSPS. FRESH BASIL—CHOPPED (2 TSP. DRIED—10mL)	30 mL
2	TBSPS. SLIVERED ALMONDS	30 mL

PARMESAN DRESSING:

1	CLOVE GARLIC—MINCED	
2	ANCHOVY FILLETS—RINSED	
2	TSPS. DIJON MUSTARD	10 mL
½	TSP. SALT	2 mL
½	TSP. GROUND PEPPER	2 mL
½	TSP. WORCESTERSHIRE SAUCE	2 mL
1	EGG YOLK	
2	TBSPS. LEMON JUICE	30 mL
1	TBSP. WHITE WINE VINEGAR	15 mL
½	CUP OLIVE OIL	125 mL
¼	CUP PARMESAN CHEESE—FRESHLY GRATED	50 mL

THAT'S ALL YOU NEED; TURN TO PAGE 85 FOR METHOD!

ASPARAGUS PASTA SALAD

THIS RECIPE CONTINUED FROM PAGE 84

NOW, LET'S SEE; COOK PASTA, DRAIN WITH COLD WATER AND SET ASIDE. COOK ASPARAGUS UNTIL TENDER CRISP. COOL. PREPARE REMAINING INGREDIENTS AND SET ASIDE. PUT DRESSING INGREDIENTS IN BLENDER AND MIX WELL. ASSEMBLE SALAD INGREDIENTS IN A LARGE BOWL, COVER WITH DRESSING AND TOSS WELL. SET IN FRIDGE AT LEAST ONE HOUR BEFORE SERVING. SERVES 6.

THOUSAND ISLAND DRESSING

ALSO GREAT ON HAMBURGERS AND REUBEN SANDWICHES.

1 CUP MAYONNAISE	250 mL
1 TBSP. VINEGAR	15 mL
¼ CUP CHILI SAUCE	50 mL
1 TSP. ONION - MINCED	5 mL
2 TBSPS. GREEN PEPPER - FINELY CHOPPED	30 mL
2 TBSPS. STUFFED OLIVES - FINELY CHOPPED	30 mL
1 EGG - HARDBOILED, COARSELY CHOPPED	

PLACE ALL INGREDIENTS IN BLENDER; MIX WELL. CHILL. WILL KEEP IN REFRIGERATOR FOR 1 TO 2 WEEKS.

Arizona Fruit Salad

GREAT WITH CHICKEN OR PORK, OR AS A LUNCHEON SALAD.

1	AVOCADO	
2	TBSPS. LIME JUICE	30 mL
1	PAPAYA	
2	ORANGES	
1	GRAPEFRUIT	
1	RED ONION	
½	POMEGRANATE (OPTIONAL)	

FOR THE DRESSING:

2	TBSPS. ORANGE JUICE	30 mL
2	TBSPS. LIME JUICE	30 mL
2	TSPS. HONEY	10 mL
¼	TSP. HOT PEPPER FLAKES	1 mL
½	CUP VEGETABLE OIL	125 mL

· 1 HEAD ROMAINE LETTUCE

PEEL AND SLICE AVOCADO. SPRINKLE WITH 1 TBSP. LIME JUICE. PEEL, SEED AND SLICE PAPAYA THINLY. SPRINKLE WITH REMAINING LIME JUICE. PEEL ORANGES AND GRAPEFRUIT. CUT FRUIT INTO SEGMENTS. CHOP RED ONION. IN A LARGE BOWL COMBINE AVOCADO, PAPAYA, ORANGE AND GRAPEFRUIT SEGMENTS AND ONION. SET ASIDE. IF USING POMEGRANATE, SCOOP OUT SEEDS AND SET ASIDE.

THIS RECIPE CONTINUED NEXT PAGE.

ARIZONA FRUIT SALAD

THIS RECIPE CONTINUED FROM PAGE 86.

TO MAKE DRESSING: WHISK ORANGE JUICE, LIME JUICE, HONEY, PEPPER FLAKES AND OIL.

BEFORE SERVING, POUR DRESSING OVER FRUIT AND TOSS WELL. SPOON ONTO LETTUCE LINED PLATTER. SPRINKLE POMEGRANATE SEEDS OVER ALL.

HAVE A LOOK AT THE PICTURE, PAGE 51.

CHART HOUSE BLEU CHEESE DRESSING

GET OUT YOUR STOP WATCH!

3/4 CUP SOUR CREAM	175 mL
1/2 TSP. DRY MUSTARD	2 mL
1/2 TSP. PEPPER	2 mL
1/2 TSP. SALT	2 mL
1/3 TSP. GARLIC POWDER	PINCH
1 TSP. WORCESTERSHIRE SAUCE	5 mL
1 1/3 CUP MAYONNAISE	325 mL
4 OZ. DANISH BLEU CHEESE - CRUMBLED	115 g

BLEND FIRST SIX INGREDIENTS FOR TWO MINUTES AT LOW SPEED. ADD MAYONNAISE AND BLEND 1/2 MINUTE AT LOW SPEED; THEN 2 MINUTES AT MEDIUM SPEED. ADD CHEESE AND BLEND AT LOW SPEED 3 TO 4 MINUTES. LET SIT 24 HOURS.
MAKES 2 1/2 CUPS.

FRUIT AND LIME CHICKEN SALAD

PERFECT FOR LUNCH - THE LADIES WILL LOVE IT!

3	TBSPS. SUGAR	45 mL
1/4	CUP VINEGAR	50 mL
2	TBSPS. LIME JUICE	30 mL
1/4	TSP. DRY MUSTARD	1 mL
	DASH OF SALT	
1/2	TSP. POPPY SEEDS	2 mL
1/2	CUP SALAD OIL	125 mL
3	CUPS CUBED COOKED CHICKEN	750 mL
1	HONEYDEW MELON	
1	CANTALOUPE	
1	HEAD LEAF LETTUCE	
1	CUP STRAWBERRIES, GREEN GRAPES OR	
	CANTALOUPE BALLS (WHICHEVER YOU LIKE)	250 mL
1/2	CUP PECAN HALVES - TOASTED	125 mL
1/2	CUP BLUEBERRIES	125 mL

COMBINE SUGAR, VINEGAR, LIME JUICE, MUSTARD, SALT AND POPPY SEEDS IN A BLENDER. WHIRL TO MIX, THEN GRADUALLY ADD OIL IN A THIN STREAM. COVER AND BLEND 2 MINUTES UNTIL DRESSING IS SLIGHTLY THICKENED. RESERVE 1/3 CUP AND POUR REMAINING DRESSING OVER CHICKEN. CHILL. TO SERVE, LINE 4 TO 6 SALAD PLATES WITH LETTUCE AND ARRANGE HONEYDEW AND CANTALOUPE WEDGES AROUND EDGE. SPOON CHICKEN INTO CENTRE. TOSS STRAWBERRIES, PECANS AND BLUEBERRIES IN RESERVED DRESSING; SPOON OVER.

MARINATED FRUIT SALAD

YOU CAN BET THAT THE FRUITS IN THIS ARE HAPPY!

1	CUP PINEAPPLE CHUNKS	250 mL
1	CUP HONEYDEW MELON CHUNKS	250 mL
1	CUP CANTALOUPE CHUNKS	250 mL
1	CUP GRAPES	250 mL
1	CUP PLUM PIECES	250 mL
2	TBSPS. GRAND MARNIER	30 mL
1	TBSP. AMARETTO	15 mL
	DASH OF LEMON JUICE	

PREPARE FRUIT PIECES. SPRINKLE FRUIT WITH THE LIQUEURS AND LEMON JUICE. MARINATE FOR TWO HOURS. SERVE IN A "SCOOPED-OUT" PINEAPPLE OR YOUR PRETTIEST GLASS BOWL. SERVE WITH FRUIT SAUCE.

FRUIT SAUCE:

2	EGG YOLKS	
¼	CUP BROWN SUGAR	50 mL
4	TBSPS. GRAND MARNIER	60 mL
1	CUP WHIPPING CREAM	250 mL

BEAT EGG YOLKS, SUGAR AND LIQUEUR UNTIL LIGHT. WHIP CREAM UNTIL STIFF AND FOLD INTO EGG MIXTURE. CHILL FOR A COUPLE OF HOURS BEFORE SERVING.

VIVA! VEGGIES

YUMMY FARE FOR COMPANY.

1	BUNCH FRESH BROCCOLI	
2	TBSPS. BUTTER	30 mL
½	LB. MUSHROOMS - SLICED	250 g
½	CUP MAYONNAISE	125 mL
½	CUP SOUR CREAM	125 mL
½	CUP PARMESAN - GRATED	125 mL
1-	14 oz. CAN ARTICHOKES - DRAINED & CUT INTO BITE-SIZED PIECES	398 mL
	SALT & PEPPER TO TASTE	
3	TOMATOES - SLICED	
¼	CUP BUTTER - MELTED	50 mL
½	CUP BREADCRUMBS	125 mL

PRE-COOK BROCCOLI UNTIL TENDER CRISP. SAUTÉ MUSHROOMS IN 2 TBSPS. BUTTER. GREASE A 9" x 13" DISH. BLEND MAYONNAISE, SOUR CREAM AND PARMESAN. MIX VEGETABLES IN SAUCE AND PLACE IN DISH. COVER WITH TOMATO SLICES. SEASON WITH SALT AND PEPPER. MIX MELTED BUTTER WITH BREADCRUMBS AND SPRINKLE OVER TOMATOES. BAKE AT 325° FOR 20 MINUTES. SERVES 10 TO 12.

THE QUICKEST WAY TO LEARN HOW TO DO-IT-YOURSELF IS TO CRITICIZE THE WAY YOUR WIFE IS DOING IT!

BAKED ASPARAGUS

SURPRISE! YOU CAN COOK ASPARAGUS IN THE OVEN WITH THE ROAST!

1 TO 1½ LBS. FRESH ASPARAGUS	450-700 g
3 TBSPS. BUTTER OR MARGARINE	45 mL
SALT & PEPPER TO TASTE	
2 TBSPS. LEMON JUICE	30 mL

PREHEAT OVEN AT 300°F. RINSE AND TRIM ASPARAGUS – DO NOT PEEL. PLACE ASPARAGUS IN A SHALLOW DISH IN ONE OR TWO LAYERS. DOT WITH BUTTER AND SPRINKLE WITH SALT AND PEPPER AND LEMON JUICE. COVER TIGHTLY WITH FOIL AND BAKE 30 MINUTES. SEE PICTURE, PAGE 121.

BEHOLD THE TURTLE – HE MAKES PROGRESS ONLY WHEN HE STICKS HIS NECK OUT!

ASPARAGUS NOODLE BAKE

MIKEY LOVES IT! - TRUST US... IT IS GOOD!

1 - 10 OZ. CAN MUSHROOM, CELERY OR	
ASPARAGUS SOUP	284 mL
1 CUP WATER	250 mL
3 CUPS CHOW MEIN NOODLES	750 mL
2 - 10 OZ. CANS ASPARAGUS TIPS - DRAINED	2 - 284 mL
3 CUPS GRATED CHEDDAR CHEESE	750 mL

COMBINE SOUP AND WATER UNTIL SMOOTH. SPOON SMALL AMOUNT INTO BOTTOM OF 1½ QT. CASSEROLE. ADD ½ THE NOODLES, ½ THE ASPARAGUS, ½ OF THE REMAINING SOUP AND ½ THE CHEESE. REPEAT THE LAYERS. BAKE AT 350° FOR 30 MINUTES. SERVES 4 TO 6.

SICILIAN BROCCOLI

A VEGETABLE YOU DARE NOT REFUSE!

1 BUNCH BROCCOLI	
4 TBSPS. BUTTER	60 mL
2 CLOVES GARLIC - MINCED	
¼ TO ½ CUP RIPE OLIVES - SLICED	50 - 125 mL
PARMESAN CHEESE - FRESHLY GRATED	

COOK BROCCOLI UNTIL TENDER CRISP. MELT BUTTER AND SAUTÉ GARLIC. ADD OLIVES AND COOK 2 MINUTES. POUR OVER BROCCOLI AND SPRINKLE WITH PARMESAN. SERVES 4.

BAKED BANANAS
IN ORANGE AND LEMON JUICE

SERVE WITH CHICKEN, HAM OR ANY CURRIED DISH.
ALSO A GREAT DESSERT SERVED OVER ICE CREAM.

3	BANANAS - PEELED (NOT FULLY RIPE)	
2	MEDIUM ORANGES - PEELED	
1/3	CUP SUGAR	75 mL
1/4	CUP BUTTER - MELTED	50 mL
2	TBSPS. ORANGE JUICE	30 mL
2	TBSPS. LEMON JUICE	30 mL

PEEL AND CUT BANANAS LENGTHWISE. PLACE IN
SHALLOW BAKING DISH. ARRANGE ORANGE SECTIONS
OVER BANANAS AND SPRINKLE WITH SUGAR. COMBINE
MELTED BUTTER AND JUICES AND POUR OVER FRUIT.
BAKE AT 450° FOR 15 MINUTES. SERVES 6.

LIFE IS LIKE CHESS - ALL THE MISTAKES
ARE THERE, WAITING TO BE MADE.

CALICO BEAN POT

A BUFFAQUE AND FAMILY BUN FIGHT BONANZA!

8 SLICES BACON	
1 CUP ONION - CHOPPED	250 mL
1 - 14 OZ. TIN GREEN BEANS - DRAINED	398 mL
1 - 14 OZ. TIN LIMA BEANS - DRAINED	398 mL
1 - 14 OZ. TIN PORK AND BEANS	398 mL
1 - 14 OZ. TIN KIDNEY BEANS - DRAINED	398 mL
¾ CUP BROWN SUGAR - FIRMLY PACKED	175 mL
½ CUP VINEGAR	125 mL
½ TSP. GARLIC SALT	2 mL
½ TSP. DRY MUSTARD	2 mL
⅛ TSP. PEPPER	1 mL

CUT BACON INTO SMALL PIECES AND COOK UNTIL CRISP. COOK ONION UNTIL SOFT. ADD REMAINING INGREDIENTS IN A LARGE CASSEROLE (2½ QT.). BAKE AT 350° FOR 1 HOUR, UNCOVERED. PERFECT WITH HAMBURGERS OR BAR-B-QUED BEEF. SERVES 12.

CAT HAIR ADHERES TO EVERYTHING —
BUT THE CAT.

FRIED CABBAGE

1   MEDIUM HEAD OF CABBAGE - SLICED
1   SPANISH ONION - SLICED
10 STRIPS OF BACON

FRY BACON UNTIL CRISP, REMOVE FROM FRYING PAN & CRUMBLE. TO REMAINING DRIPPINGS, ADD ONION AND FRY UNTIL LIMP, THEN ADD CABBAGE GRADUALLY AND COOK UNTIL SOFT, STIRRING FREQUENTLY. BEFORE SERVING, ADD CRUMBLED BACON. SERVE WITH PEROGIES, SAUSAGE OR HAM. SERVES 6 TO 8.

SPEEDY BAKED BEANS

SERVE WITH QUICK MOLASSES BROWN BREAD, PAGE 23

1 - 28 OZ. CAN PORK & BEANS IN TOMATO SAUCE	796 mL
1/4 CUP BROWN SUGAR - PACKED	50 mL
1/4 CUP KETCHUP	50 mL
3 TBSPS. FROZEN ORANGE JUICE CONCENTRATE	45 mL
1 TBSP. DRIED MINCED ONION	15 mL
1 TBSP. WORCESTERSHIRE SAUCE	15 mL
SALT & PEPPER - TO TASTE	
1 TSP. DRY MUSTARD	5 mL

PLACE ALL INGREDIENTS IN 2 QT. CASSEROLE. MIX WELL. BAKE AT 350° FOR 35 TO 40 MINUTES; OR HEAT THOROUGHLY ON STOVE TOP OR MICROWAVE. SERVES 4.

CURRIED CAULIFLOWER

MAKE AHEAD AND FREEZE.

4	CUPS CAULIFLOWER (1 HEAD)	1 L
1	TBSP. MILK	15 mL
1 - 10 oz.	CAN CREAM OF CHICKEN SOUP	284 mL
¼	CUP MAYONNAISE	50 mL
½	CUP CHEDDAR CHEESE - GRATED	125 mL
1	TSP. CURRY POWDER	5 mL
2	TBSPS. BUTTER - MELTED	30 mL
1	CUP CRACKER CRUMBS	250 mL

COOK CAULIFLOWER UNTIL TENDER CRISP AND SET IN LARGE CASSEROLE DISH. COMBINE MILK, CHICKEN SOUP, MAYONNAISE, CHEESE AND CURRY POWDER AND POUR OVER CAULIFLOWER. MIX MELTED BUTTER AND CRACKER CRUMBS AND SPRINKLE OVER ALL. BAKE AT 350° FOR 30 MINUTES. SERVES 6.

THERE'S NOTHING WRONG WITH TEENAGERS THAT REASONING WON'T AGGRAVATE!

FLUFFY BAKED POTATOES

6	BAKING POTATOES	
2	TBSPS. BUTTER	30 mL
1/2	CUP HOT MILK	125 mL
1	TSP. SALT	5 mL
1/4	TSP. PEPPER	1 mL
1	TSP. BAKING POWDER	5 mL
JUST A PINCH—NUTMEG		
2	EGG YOLKS (PLACE IN SEPARATE BOWLS)	
2	EGG WHITES	
1/2	CUP SWISS CHEESE — FINELY GRATED	125 mL
2	TBSPS. ONIONS — GRATED (OPTIONAL)	30 mL
1	TBSP. WATER	15 mL

PREHEAT OVEN TO 425°. PRICK AND BAKE POTATOES FOR 1 HOUR. CUT THIN SLICE FROM TOP HALF OF EACH POTATO AND DISCARD. SCOOP POTATO PULP INTO BOWL WITH TEASPOON, BEING CAREFUL NOT TO BREAK SKIN. MASH PULP WELL (USE BEATER). ADD BUTTER, MILK, SALT, PEPPER, BAKING POWDER, NUTMEG AND ONE EGG YOLK AND ONION. WHIP UNTIL FLUFFY. BEAT EGG WHITES UNTIL STIFF AND FOLD INTO MIXTURE. MIX IN CHEESE AND PILE BACK INTO POTATO SKINS. BEAT REMAINING EGG YOLK WITH WATER. BRUSH OVER EACH POTATO. SET IN PAN AND BAKE 15 MINUTES AT 400°. SERVES 6.

POTATOES ROSTI

POTATOES - SCRUBBED, UNPEELED
2 TBSPS. BUTTER   30 mL
2 TBSPS. SALAD OIL   30 mL
SEASONING SALT TO TASTE

PREPARE POTATOES USING A MELON BALLER (ALLOW
8 TO 10 BALLS PER PERSON) - (LEFT OVER POTATOES
MAY BE CHOPPED AND FROZEN FOR LATER USE AS
HASH BROWNS). PAR BOIL BALLS FOR 5 MINUTES.
DRAIN. PREHEAT OVEN TO 350°. PUT BUTTER AND OIL
IN ROASTING PAN AND HEAT FOR 10 MINUTES; ADD
POTATOES AND BAKE 45 MINUTES, STIRRING OFTEN.
DRAIN ON PAPER TOWEL. SPRINKLE WITH SALT. THESE
MAY ALSO BE COOKED IN AN ELECTRIC FRY PAN.
SEE PICTURE, PAGE 121.

A SPILLED DRINK FLOWS IN THE DIRECTION
OF THE MOST EXPENSIVE DRESS!

DILL AND PARMESAN TOMATOES

A QUICK WAY TO PERK UP A MIDWEEK MEAL.

3	MEDIUM TOMATOES	
2	TBSPS. BUTTER	30 mL
½	CUP BREADCRUMBS (KEEP A BAG IN THE FREEZER)	125mL
3	TSPS. FRESH CHOPPED DILL (KEEPS WELL IN FREEZER)	
	OR 1½ TSP. DRIED DILL	15 OR 7 mL

SALT & PEPPER TO TASTE
GRATED PARMESAN CHEESE

CUT EACH TOMATO INTO 4 SLICES AND PLACE ON A COOKIE SHEET. MELT BUTTER, ADD BREADCRUMBS, DILL, SALT AND PEPPER. SPOON MIXTURE ONTO EACH TOMATO SLICE. SPRINKLE WITH LOTS OF PARMESAN CHEESE. PLACE IN COLD OVEN UNDER BROILER (NOT TOO CLOSE) AND TURN ON BROILER. KEEP AN EYE ON IT — CHEESE TURNS GOLDEN AND CRUSTY IN ABOUT 5 MINUTES. SEE PICTURE, PAGE 121.

AT FIRST I WAS HESITANT — BUT NOW,
I'M NOT SO SURE.

SPINACH OR BROCCOLI TIMBALES

A SPECIAL COMPANY VEGETABLE. LOOKS ATTRACTIVE ON A PLATTER SERVED WITH DILL & PARMESAN TOMATOES.

2	PKGS. - 10 OZ. FROZEN SPINACH OR BROCCOLI	2-300 g
½	CUP CHOPPED GREEN ONIONS	125 mL
3	TBSPS. BUTTER	45 mL
4	EGGS - BEATEN	
1½	CUPS HALF 'N' HALF CREAM	375 mL
¾	CUP DRY BREADCRUMBS	175 mL
½	CUP GRATED PARMESAN CHEESE	125 mL
½	TSP. SALT	2 mL
¼	TSP. PEPPER	1 mL
⅛	TSP. NUTMEG	.5 mL

GREASE 16 LARGE MUFFIN TINS. COOK SPINACH OR BROCCOLI. DRAIN WELL (SPIN SPINACH IN SALAD SPINNER). CHOP. SAUTÉ ONIONS IN BUTTER UNTIL SOFT; COMBINE WITH REMAINING INGREDIENTS. FILL MUFFIN TINS AND BAKE 20 TO 25 MINUTES AT 350° OR UNTIL A TOOTHPICK COMES OUT CLEAN. UNMOLD AND TURN RIGHT SIDE UP. THESE LITTLE MARVELS WILL EVEN SUFFER THE INDIGNITY OF REHEATING. SERVES 8.

TOO MUCH OF A GOOD THING IS WONDERFUL!

ÉPINARDS, EH!!

5	MEDIUM CARROTS - PEELED & SLICED	
1	MEDIUM ONION - SLICED	
1½	TBSPS. BUTTER	22 mL
1½	TBSPS. FLOUR	22 mL
¾	CUP MILK	175 mL
½	CUP VELVEETA CHEESE - CUBED	125 mL
½	CUP CHEDDAR CHEESE - GRATED	125 mL
1	- 10 oz. PKG. FROZEN LEAF SPINACH - THAWED & DRAINED	300 g
¼	TSP. SALT	1 mL
¼	TSP. PEPPER	1 mL

COOK CARROTS AND ONION IN SMALL AMOUNT OF WATER UNTIL TENDER CRISP - ABOUT 8 MINUTES. DRAIN. IN A SAUCEPAN, MELT BUTTER AND BLEND IN FLOUR GRADUALLY. STIR IN MILK AND ADD CHEESES. COOK AND STIR UNTIL THICK. PLACE HALF THE SPINACH IN 1 QT. CASSEROLE. COVER WITH HALF THE CARROTS AND ONION. COVER WITH THE CHEESE SAUCE. REPEAT VEGETABLES. BAKE, COVERED, AT 350° FOR 15 TO 20 MINUTES. SERVES 6.

SPAGHETTI SQUASH PRIMAVERA

A WONDERFUL VEGETARIAN DINNER - OR - IF YOU'RE NOT INTO THAT, SERVE WITH BEEF, BOOZE AND A GOOD STOGIE!

1	MEDIUM SPAGHETTI SQUASH	
1	CUP BUTTER	250 mL
2	MEDIUM ONIONS - DICED	
½	LB. MUSHROOMS - SLICED	250 g
1	SMALL CLOVE GARLIC - MINCED	
1½	CUPS BROCCOLI FLOWERETTES	375 mL
1	CUP PEAS	250 mL
1	MEDIUM ZUCCHINI - SLICED	
4	CARROTS - CUT DIAGONALLY	
1½	CUP WHIPPING CREAM	375 mL
½	CUP CHICKEN STOCK	125 mL
¼	CUP FRESH BASIL LEAVES OR	50 mL
1	TBSP. DRIED BASIL	OR 15 mL
1	SWEET RED PEPPER - SLICED	
6	GREEN ONIONS - CHOPPED	
12	CHERRY TOMATOES	
1½	CUPS PARMESAN - GRATED	375 mL

CUT SQUASH IN HALF LENGTHWISE AND REMOVE SEEDS. PLACE CUT SIDE DOWN IN A BAKING DISH, ADD 1" OF WATER AND BAKE AT 375° FOR ONE HOUR. PRICK SQUASH WITH A SKEWER TO TEST DONENESS. MELT BUTTER IN A LARGE FRYING PAN AND SAUTÉ ONIONS, MUSHROOMS AND GARLIC UNTIL ONIONS ARE SOFT.

THERE'S MORE - SEE NEXT PAGE.

PICTURED ON OVERLEAF:

SWEET AND SPICY CASHEW CHICKEN—
PAGE 148

SPAGHETTI SQUASH PRIMAVERA

THIS RECIPE CONTINUED FROM PAGE 102.

ADD BROCCOLI, PEAS, ZUCCHINI AND CARROTS. STIR. ADD CREAM, STOCK AND BASIL. BOIL BRISKLY TO EVAPORATE SAUCE A LITTLE — ABOUT 2 MINUTES. ADD RED PEPPER, GREEN ONIONS, CHERRY TOMATOES AND CHEESE. HEAT THOROUGHLY. USING A FORK, SCRAPE STRANDS OF SQUASH INTO A LARGE, HOT, SHALLOW CASSEROLE. TOP IMMEDIATELY WITH HOT VEGETABLE MIXTURE. SERVE WITH EXTRA PARMESAN CHEESE. SERVES 10 TO 12.

CHEESE MARINATED ONIONS

A REAL ZINGER WITH ROAST BEEF OR HAMBURGERS.

3	OZ. BLUE CHEESE — CRUMBLED	57 g
1/4	CUP SALAD OIL	50 mL
2	TBSPS. LEMON JUICE	30 mL
2	TSPS. SUGAR	10 mL
	SALT AND PEPPER TO TASTE	
2	LARGE ONIONS — THINLY SLICED AND SEPARATED INTO RINGS	

MIX FIRST FIVE INGREDIENTS AND POUR OVER ONION RINGS. COVER AND CHILL SEVERAL HOURS.

EVER SEE A "FULL" ONION— WELL, HERE'S THREE OF THEM.

3	MEDIUM SPANISH ONIONS — PEELED	
1	LB. FRESH BROCCOLI	500 g
½	CUP GRATED PARMESAN CHEESE	125 mL
⅓	CUP MAYONNAISE	75 mL
2	TSPS. LEMON JUICE	10 mL

PREHEAT OVEN TO 375°. CUT THE ONIONS IN HALF CROSSWISE. GENTLY PARBOIL IN SALTED WATER FOR 10 TO 12 MINUTES. DRAIN. REMOVE CENTRES LEAVING ¾" WALLS. CHOP CENTRE PORTIONS TO EQUAL 1 CUP. COOK BROCCOLI TOPS UNTIL TENDER CRISP; CHOP. COMBINE WITH CHOPPED ONION, CHEESE, MAYONNAISE AND LEMON JUICE. MOUND BROCCOLI MIXTURE IN THE ONION HALVES. BAKE, UNCOVERED, IN A BUTTERED, SHALLOW CASSEROLE FOR 20 MINUTES. SERVES 6, BUT, DON'T EXPECT A DATE FOR TWO OR THREE DAYS! SEE PICTURE, PAGE 121.

DON'T YOU WISH THAT ALL THOSE PEOPLE TRYING TO FIND THEMSELVES WOULD JUST GET LOST!

POTATO LATKES

OY VEY! POTATO PANCAKES AND TASTY TOO!
CAN BE MADE THE NIGHT BEFORE AND REFRIED OR
MICROWAVED FOR BRUNCH. IF YOU HAVE LEFTOVERS,
JUST FREEZE BETWEEN LAYERS OF WAXED PAPER.

3 LARGE POTATOES - PEELED & GRATED	
1/2 MEDIUM ONION - GRATED	
JUICE OF ONE LEMON	
6 EGGS	
1/2 CUP FLOUR	125 mL
1/2 CUP OIL	125 mL
2 TBSPS. PARSLEY	30 mL
1 TSP. SALT	5 mL
1/2 TSP. PEPPER	2 mL
1/8 TSP. GARLIC POWDER	.5 mL
APPLESAUCE & SOUR CREAM	

PLACE POTATOES AND ONION IN BOWL AND TOSS
WITH LEMON JUICE; COVER WITH COLD WATER.
BEAT TOGETHER EGGS, FLOUR, OIL, PARSLEY, SALT,
PEPPER AND GARLIC POWDER. ADD WELL DRAINED
POTATO MIXTURE AND MIX WELL. BATTER WILL BE
SOUPY! DROP BY TABLESPOONS ONTO A LIGHTLY
BUTTERED FRYPAN, SPREADING OUT SLIGHTLY.
FRY OVER MEDIUM HEAT UNTIL GOLDEN BROWN
ON EACH SIDE. MAKES AT LEAST 30. SERVE WITH
APPLESAUCE AND SOUR CREAM. DEE LISH!

PERFECT PARSNIPS

IF YOU ARE A DEVOTEE, THESE ARE:
PRESENTABLE, PALATABLE AND POSITIVELY A SNAP.

3 PARSNIPS-PEELED & SLICED IN MATCHSTICKS	
1 CARROT (FOR COLOUR)-PEELED & SLICED IN MATCHSTICKS	
3 TBSPS. BUTTER	45 mL
1 TBSP. LEMON JUICE	15 mL
2 TSPS. FRESH DILL...OR...	10 mL
1 TSP. DRIED DILL	5 mL

STIR FRY PARSNIPS AND CARROTS IN BUTTER OVER MEDIUM HIGH HEAT 3 TO 4 MINUTES UNTIL TENDER CRISP. REMOVE TO CASSEROLE DISH AND SPRINKLE WITH LEMON JUICE AND DILL. SERVES 4-6.
YOU WILL WANT TO SEE THE PICTURE, PAGE 121.

THERE'S NO SENSE IN ADVERTISING YOUR TROUBLES— THERE'S NO MARKET FOR THEM.

RICE WITH MUSHROOMS AND PINE NUTS

1	CUP BOILING WATER	250 mL
1/3	CUP RAISINS	75 mL
6	TBSPS. BUTTER	90 mL
1	TBSP. OLIVE OIL	15 mL
1/2	ONION - CHOPPED	
1	CUP LONG GRAIN RICE - UNCOOKED	250 mL
2	CHICKEN BOUILLON CUBES	
2	CUPS BOILING WATER	500 mL
1	CUP FRESH MUSHROOMS - SLICED	250 mL
1/4	CUP PINE NUTS	50 mL
	SALT & PEPPER	

PREHEAT OVEN TO 375°. POUR 1 CUP BOILING WATER OVER RAISINS. SET ASIDE. MELT 3 TBSPS. BUTTER IN OVEN PROOF BAKING DISH, ADD OIL AND SAUTÉ ONION UNTIL SOFT. ADD UNCOOKED RICE AND STIR 2 TO 3 MINUTES. DISSOLVE CUBES IN THE LAST 2 CUPS BOILING WATER AND POUR OVER RICE. COVER, PLACE IN OVEN AND BAKE 15 TO 20 MINUTES OR UNTIL LIQUID IS ABSORBED. SAUTÉ MUSHROOMS AND PINE NUTS IN 3 TBSPS. BUTTER FOR 5 MINUTES. DRAIN RAISINS. ADD MUSHROOMS, RAISINS, PINE NUTS AND SALT AND PEPPER TO COOKED RICE. TOSS WITH A FORK. SERVES 6.

PUT YOUR TROUBLES IN A POCKET WITH A HOLE IN IT.

WILD BUFFET RICE!

MAKES LOTS AND IS PERFECT WITH ANY MEAT.

1 CUP WILD RICE	250 mL
1 - 10 oz. CAN CHICKEN BROTH	284 mL
1 - 10 oz. CAN WATER	284 mL
10 PORK SAUSAGES - BROWNED, DRAINED AND	
CUT INTO SMALL PIECES	
1/2 LB. FRESH MUSHROOMS - SLICED	250 g
1 LARGE ONION - FINELY CHOPPED	
2 TBSPS. FLOUR	30 mL
1 CUP WHIPPING CREAM	250 mL
1 TSP. SALT	5 mL
1/4 TSP. OREGANO	1 mL
1/4 TSP. SAGE	1 mL
1/4 TSP. MARJORAM	1 mL
1/4 TSP. THYME	1 mL
1/2 CUP BLANCHED ALMONDS - SLIVERED	125 mL

WASH WILD RICE AND COMBINE WITH BROTH AND WATER IN A LARGE, COVERED POT. BRING TO BOIL AND REDUCE HEAT TO A SLOW BOIL FOR 1 HOUR OR UNTIL RICE BEGINS TO OPEN AND IS SOFT. SO FAR - SO GOOD. NOW, SAUTÉ ONION AND MUSHROOMS IN SKILLET AFTER SAUSAGE IS COOKED. ADD SAUSAGE AND ONION MIXTURE TO RICE. IN SAME SKILLET ON MEDIUM HEAT COMBINE FLOUR AND CREAM, STIRRING CONSTANTLY TO MAKE A CREAMY SAUCE, ADDING MORE CREAM OR WATER IF NECESSARY. (THIS RECIPE CONTINUED NEXT PAGE.)

WILD BUFFET RICE!

THIS RECIPE CONTINUED FROM PAGE 110.

BRING MIXTURE TO A BOIL FOR THREE MINUTES. ADD SEASONINGS. POUR RICE MIXTURE, SAUCE AND ALMONDS INTO LARGE CASSEROLE. MIX WELL AND BAKE AT 350° FOR 30 MINUTES. SERVES 10 TO 12.

OVEN BAKED WILD RICE

SERVE WITH BEEF EXTRAORDINAIRE AND SAUCE DIANE, PAGE 118.

1½ CUPS WILD RICE	375 mL
½ CUP BUTTER	125 mL
1- 4 OZ. CAN WATER CHESTNUTS	115 mL
2 CUPS FRESH MUSHROOMS - SLICED	500 mL
4- 10 OZ. CANS CONSOMMÉ - UNDILUTED	4-284 mL

SOAK WILD RICE OVERNIGHT IN A GENEROUS AMOUNT OF WATER. DRAIN. MELT BUTTER IN A 2 QT. CASSEROLE. ADD RICE, WATER CHESTNUTS AND MUSHROOMS AND STIR. POUR IN CONSOMMÉ. LET STAND UNTIL READY TO BAKE. THIS MIXTURE WILL BE RUNNY - BUT DON'T PANIC - IN 1½ TO 2 HOURS, BAKED AT 325° YOU'LL HAVE FLUFFY RICE. SERVES 8.

Italian Zucchini

8 MEDIUM ZUCCHINI	
3 MEDIUM ONIONS	
1 CLOVE GARLIC - CHOPPED	
½ CUP OIL	125 mL
1-28 oz. CAN TOMATOES	796 mL
SALT & PEPPER TO TASTE	
2 TSPS. OREGANO	10 mL
1 TBSP. WINE VINEGAR	15 mL
3 TBSPS. PARMESAN CHEESE	45 mL

SLICE ZUCCHINI AND ARRANGE IN A 3 QT. CASSEROLE. SAUTÉ ONIONS AND GARLIC IN OIL UNTIL LIGHTLY BROWN AND TENDER. ADD TOMATOES, SALT, PEPPER, OREGANO AND VINEGAR. HEAT TO BOILING, THEN SIMMER FOR TWO MINUTES. POUR TOMATO-ONION MIXTURE OVER ZUCCHINI. TOP WITH GRATED CHEESE. BAKE AT 400° FOR ½ HOUR, OR UNTIL TENDER. SERVES 8 TO 10.

BIG TOE - A DEVICE FOR LOCATING SHARP OBJECTS IN THE DARK!

2 LBS. GROUND BEEF	1 kg
1 ONION - CHOPPED	
1 PKG. TACO SEASONING	33 g
1/4 TSP. PEPPER	1 mL
1/4 TSP. OREGANO	1 mL
PARSLEY, TO TASTE	
1 CUP SOUR CREAM	250 mL
2 LBS. MONTEREY JACK CHEESE - SHREDDED	1 kg
3/4 CUP TACO SAUCE	175 mL
20 FLOUR TORTILLA SHELLS	

BROWN GROUND BEEF AND ONIONS. ADD TACO SEASONING, PEPPER, OREGANO, PARSLEY AND SOUR CREAM. ADD 1/2 THE CHEESE AND 1/2 THE TACO SAUCE, MIXING WELL. PLACE 2 OR MORE TABLESPOONS OF MIXTURE ON TORTILLA SHELL AND ROLL UP. PLACE SEAM SIDE DOWN IN 9" x 13" CASSEROLE DISH. * TOP WITH REMAINING CHEESE AND TACO SAUCE. BAKE AT 350° FOR 15 MINUTES OR UNTIL CHEESE MELTS AND IS HEATED THROUGH.

* THIS FREEZES WELL. FOR INDIVIDUAL SERVINGS, WRAP EACH BURRITO IN PLASTIC WRAP AND FREEZE. DO NOT ADD THE REMAINING CHEESE AND TACO SAUCE UNTIL READY TO BAKE. MAKES 20.

CABBAGE ROLL CASSEROLE

A FAST ALTERNATIVE FOR CABBAGE ROLLS!

1½ LBS. GROUND BEEF	750 g
2 MEDIUM ONIONS - CHOPPED	
1 CLOVE GARLIC - MINCED	
1 TSP. SALT	5 mL
¼ TSP. PEPPER	1 mL
1 - 14 oz. CAN TOMATO SAUCE	398 mL
1 CAN WATER	
½ CUP UNCOOKED LONG GRAIN RICE	125 mL
4 CUPS CABBAGE - SHREDDED	1 L
SOUR CREAM	

BROWN BEEF, ONIONS, GARLIC, SALT, PEPPER, TOMATO SAUCE AND WATER. BRING TO A BOIL AND STIR IN RICE. COVER AND SIMMER FOR 20 MINUTES. PLACE ½ OF THE CABBAGE IN A GREASED BAKING DISH; COVER WITH ½ THE RICE MIXTURE. REPEAT LAYERS. COVER AND BAKE IN 350° OVEN FOR ONE HOUR. SERVE WITH SOUR CREAM. MAY BE REFRIGERATED BEFORE BAKING. SERVES 6.

PEOPLE WHO NEVER PLAY GOLF LIE ABOUT OTHER THINGS.

TACO PIE

1 LB. GROUND BEEF	500 g
½ CUP ONION – CHOPPED	125 mL
1 – 1¼ OZ. PKG. TACO SEASONING	33 g
1 – 4 OZ. CAN GREEN CHILIES – CHOPPED	114 mL
1¼ CUP MILK	300 mL
¾ CUP BISCUIT MIX	175 mL
3 EGGS	
2 TOMATOES – SLICED	
1 CUP MOZZARELLA OR CHEDDAR CHEESE – GRATED	

SALSA

SHREDDED LETTUCE, SOUR CREAM,
AVOCADOS OR OLIVES

BROWN BEEF AND ONION. DRAIN. STIR IN TACO SEASONING. SPREAD ON BOTTOM OF 10" PIE PLATE. SPRINKLE WITH CHILIES. IN BLENDER BEAT MILK, BISCUIT MIX AND EGGS UNTIL SMOOTH. POUR OVER MEAT MIXTURE. BAKE 25 MINUTES AT 400°. TOP WITH TOMATO SLICES. SPRINKLE WITH GRATED CHEESE. BAKE 5 MINUTES MORE OR UNTIL CHEESE MELTS. CUT IN WEDGES AND SERVE WITH SALSA AND TOPPINGS. SERVES 6.

MEN SHOULD COME WITH DIRECTIONS

SHORT-CUT STROGANOFF

THIS HAS TO BE GOOD — IT'S GOT WINE IN IT!

2	LBS. STEWING BEEF	1 kg
	FLOUR, SALT, PEPPER & GARLIC POWDER TO TASTE	
2	TBSPS. OIL	30 mL
1 - 10 oz.	CAN CREAM OF MUSHROOM SOUP	284 mL
½	CUP DRY WHITE WINE	125 mL
1	MEDIUM ONION - CHOPPED	
1 - 10 oz.	CAN SLICED MUSHROOMS	284 mL

DREDGE BEEF IN SEASONED FLOUR AND BROWN IN OIL. MIX SOUP, WINE, ONION AND MUSHROOMS IN A CASSEROLE. ADD BROWNED BEEF. COVER WITH A TIGHT FITTING LID AND BAKE AT 300° FOR 3 TO 4 HOURS. SERVE OVER RICE OR NOODLES. CAESAR SALAD (PAGE 121 - "THE BEST OF BRIDGE") IS GREAT WITH THIS DINNER. SERVES 4 TO 6.

IF AT FIRST YOU DON'T SUCCEED - LOWER YOUR STANDARDS

GREEK RIBS

DON'T ASK! JUST MAKE THEM.

SEASONING SALT
GARLIC SALT
TARRAGON OR OREGANO
LEMON JUICE
SPARERIBS

PLACE RIBS ON BROILING PAN. BROIL ON BOTH SIDES. POUR OFF FAT. SPRINKLE TO YOUR HEARTS CONTENT WITH FIRST THREE INGREDIENTS. POUR OVER LEMON JUICE AND BAKE AT 350° FOR 30 TO 40 MINUTES. THESE ARE A LOW CALORIE WAY TO ENJOY EVERYONE'S FAVOURITE!

IF YOU'RE <u>NOT</u> COUNTING, SERVE WITH FLUFFY BAKED POTATOES, PAGE 97 OR CHEESY SCALLOPED POTATOES, ("ENJOY!" PAGE 82) AND A TOSSED GREEN SALAD.

TO SLOW DOWN TRAFFIC, LET THE POST OFFICE HANDLE IT.

BEEF EXTRAORDINAIRE
WITH SAUCE DIANE

WHEN THE BOSS COMES TO DINNER......

4	LBS. BEEF TENDERLOIN	2 kg
½	CUP BUTTER – MELTED	125 mL
¾	LB. MUSHROOMS – SLICED	340 g
1½	CUPS GREEN ONIONS – SLICED	375 mL
2	TSPS. DRY MUSTARD	10 mL
1	TBSP. LEMON JUICE	15 mL
1	TBSP. WORCESTERSHIRE SAUCE	15 mL
1	TSP. SALT	5 mL

LEAVE TENDERLOIN IN WHOLE PIECE. PLACE IN PAN ON RACK IN 500° OVEN FOR 30 MINUTES. USE MEAT THERMOMETER – 30 MINUTES WILL COOK BEEF TO MEDIUM STAGE. WHILE MEAT IS COOKING, SAUTÉ THE MUSHROOMS AND GREEN ONIONS IN THE MELTED BUTTER WITH MUSTARD FOR 5 MINUTES. ADD REMAINING INGREDIENTS AND COOK AN ADDITIONAL 5 MINUTES. KEEP WARM ON BACK OF STOVE. CUT MEAT INTO THICK SLICES. SERVE WITH SAUCE AND OVEN BAKED WILD RICE, (SEE PAGE 111). SERVES 8. SEE PICTURE, PAGE 121.

SO, DID YOU GET THE RAISE?

I MAY RISE – BUT I REFUSE TO SHINE!

LIVER STIR-FRY

A SURE-FIRE STIR-FRYER.

1	LB. CALVES LIVER	500 g
1	TSP. CORNSTARCH	5 mL
1	CLOVE GARLIC - MINCED	
1	TBSP. BRANDY (OPTIONAL)	15 mL
2	TBSPS. OIL	30 mL
1	MEDIUM ONION - THINLY SLICED	
2	CUPS MUSHROOMS - THINLY SLICED	500 mL
4	GREEN ONIONS - SLICED	
1	TBSP. SOY SAUCE	15 mL

SLICE LIVER INTO THIN STRIPS. MIX WITH CORNSTARCH, GARLIC AND BRANDY. BROWN QUICKLY IN HOT OIL. ADD ONIONS AND MUSHROOMS. STIR FRY UNTIL LIMP (NOT YOU, THE FOOD). ADD GREEN ONIONS AND SOY SAUCE. COOK AND STIR FOR 2 TO 3 MINUTES. SERVES 4.

A WOMAN'S PLACE IS IN THE MALL!

GINGER FRIED BEEF

CONFUCIUS SAY... "BEST OF BRIDGE HAS VERY GOOD CHINESE RECIPE"!

1	LB. FLANK STEAK	500 g
2	EGGS - BEATEN	
¾	CUP CORNSTARCH	175 mL
½	CUP WATER	125 mL
	VEGETABLE OIL	
⅔	CUP CARROTS - GRATED	150 mL
2	TBSPS. GREEN ONION - CHOPPED	30 mL
4	TBSPS. FRESH GINGER ROOT - FINELY CHOPPED	60 mL
4	CLOVES GARLIC - CHOPPED	
3	TBSPS. SOYA SAUCE	45 mL
2	TBSPS. COOKING WINE - RED OR WHITE	30 mL
2	TBSPS. WHITE VINEGAR	30 mL
1	TBSP. SESAME OIL	15 mL
½	CUP SUGAR	125 mL

DASH - CRUSHED CHILIES (FLAKES) OPTIONAL

SLICE STEAK WHILE PARTIALLY FROZEN INTO NARROW STRIPS. MIX BEEF AND EGGS. DISSOLVE CORNSTARCH IN WATER AND MIX WITH BEEF. POUR AMPLE OIL IN WOK. HEAT TO BOILING HOT, BUT NOT SMOKING. ADD BEEF TO OIL, ¼ AT A TIME. SEPARATE WITH A FORK (OR CHOPSTICKS IF YOU'RE TALENTED) AND COOK, STIRRING FREQUENTLY UNTIL CRISPY. REMOVE, DRAIN AND SET ASIDE.*

*THIS MUCH CAN BE DONE IN ADVANCE - FOR THE REST SEE NEXT PAGE.

PICTURED ON OVERLEAF:

BEEF EXTRAORDINAIRE WITH SAUCE DIANE-
PAGE 118

PERFECT PARSNIPS - PAGE 108

POTATOES ROSTI - PAGE 98

BAKED ASPARAGUS - PAGE 91

ONIONS STUFFED WITH BROCCOLI - PAGE 106

DILL AND PARMESAN TOMATOES - PAGE 99

GINGER FRIED BEEF

THE 'RECIPE' CONTINUED FROM PAGE 120.

PUT 1 TBSP. OIL IN WOK. ADD CARROTS, ONION, GINGER AND GARLIC AND STIR FRY OVER HIGH HEAT. ADD REMAINING INGREDIENTS AND BRING TO A BOIL. ADD BEEF, MIX WELL AND SERVE. IF YOUR STEAK IS OVER ONE POUND, COOK IT ALL ANYWAY. SERVE WITH STEAMED RICE - OF COURSE. SERVES 4.

UNATTENDED ROAST BEEF

PARTY TIME! YOU NEVER NEED TO WORRY AGAIN ABOUT OVER OR UNDER COOKING YOUR ROAST!

8 TO 14 LBS. ROLLED ROAST OF BEEF   4 TO 7 KG
- BONES REMOVED

REMOVE BEEF FROM REFRIGERATOR AT LEAST 1 HOUR BEFORE COOKING. PREHEAT OVEN TO 500°. SPRINKLE ROAST LIBERALLY WITH PEPPER, SALT AND GARLIC POWDER. PLACE ON A RACK IN A WARM ROASTING PAN. ROAST FOR 20 MINUTES AT 500°, THEN TURN OVEN DOWN TO LOWEST SETTING. LEAVE FOR 8 HOURS - AND DON'T PEEK! TAPE OVEN DOOR SO YOU WON'T FORGET. BEFORE SERVING, TURN OVEN TO 350° FOR 20 MINUTES. GUARANTEED TO MELT IN YOUR MOUTH AND LIQUIDATE YOUR BANK ACCOUNT.

CREAMY DILLED SNAPPER

2	LBS. RED SNAPPER (FRESH IS BEST)	1 kg
	SALT & PEPPER	
1	CUP SOUR CREAM...OR...PLAIN YOGURT	250 mL
½	CUP MAYONNAISE	125 mL
4	TBSPS. LEMON JUICE	60 mL
4	TBSPS. FLOUR	60 mL
½	TSP. DRIED DILL WEED (1 TSP. IF FRESH)	2 mL
	PAPRIKA	

CUT FISH INTO SERVING-SIZED PIECES AND ARRANGE IN SINGLE LAYER IN A 9" x 13" BAKING DISH. SPRINKLE LIGHTLY WITH SALT AND PEPPER. IN A BOWL COMBINE THE NEXT FIVE INGREDIENTS; STIR UNTIL SMOOTH AND WELL BLENDED. SPREAD OVER FISH. COVER AND BAKE AT 400° FOR 20 TO 25 MINUTES OR UNTIL FLESH IS OPAQUE AND FLAKES. SPRINKLE WITH PAPRIKA. SERVES 6. SERVE WITH RICE, SPINACH SALAD AND BREAD STICKS.

I'M STUBBORN ONLY WHEN I DON'T GET MY WAY.

O-SOLE-O-MIO
OR SOLE FOR FOUR!

OH YUMMY!

4 FRESH SOLE FILLETS	
4 TSPS. BUTTER	20mL
4 TBSPS. FROZEN ORANGE CONCENTRATE	60mL
4 GREEN ONIONS - CHOPPED	
SALT & PEPPER TO TASTE	

PREHEAT OVEN TO 450°. LAY 4 PIECES OF FOIL, EACH 10" LONG, ON COUNTER, SHINY-SIDE UP. PLACE ONE FILLET IN CENTRE OF EACH. PLACE 1 TSP. BUTTER, 1 TBSP. ORANGE CONCENTRATE AND CHOPPED GREEN ONION ON EACH. WRAP AND SEAL. PLACE ON BAKING SHEET. BAKE FOR 15 MINUTES. THE EXTRA JUICE MAKES A NICE SAUCE. SERVE WITH RICE AND MANDARIN ORANGE SALAD - 'ENJOY!' PAGE 71.

WHEN YOU CROSS A GORILLA AND A MINK YOU GET A BEAUTIFUL COAT - BUT THE SLEEVES ARE TOO LONG!

WINE POACHED HALIBUT

3- 1 LB. HALIBUT STEAKS - CUT IN HALF	1.5 kg
½ CUP DRY WHITE WINE	125 mL
3 TBSPS. LEMON JUICE	45 mL
4 TBSPS. MARGARINE OR BUTTER	60 mL
½ CUP GREEN ONION - THINLY SLICED	125 mL
SALT AND PEPPER	

ARRANGE STEAK HALVES SIDE BY SIDE IN A GREASED 9" x 13" BAKING DISH. POUR WINE AND LEMON JUICE OVER FISH AND COVER DISH TIGHTLY WITH FOIL. BAKE AT 375° FOR 15 MINUTES. REMOVE FISH TO PLATTER AND KEEP WARM. POUR JUICE FROM FISH INTO SMALL SAUCEPAN, ADD BUTTER AND ONIONS, BRING TO BOIL AND REDUCE LIQUID TO ⅔ CUP. SEASON WITH SALT AND PEPPER. SPOON OVER FISH. SERVE WITH GREEN BEANS, RICE AND DILLED PARMESAN TOMATOES, PAGE 99 AND, OF COURSE, THE REST OF THE WINE. SERVES 6.

I GAVE UP SMOKING, DRINKING AND SEX —
IT WAS THE WORST HOUR OF MY LIFE!

BAKED FISH MOZZARELLA

THIS IS SO GOOD! SERVES 5-6 OR SERVE AT 5 TO 6.

2 LBS. THICK FLOUNDER OR SOLE FILLETS (FRESH IS BEST)	900 g
1 CUP MOZZARELLA CHEESE - SHREDDED	250 mL
1 LARGE TOMATO - THINLY SLICED	
1/2 TO 1 TSP. DRIED OREGANO	2-5 mL
SALT, FRESHLY GROUND PEPPER & GARLIC SALT	

PREHEAT OVEN TO 375°. BUTTER A 9" x 13" BAKING DISH. RINSE FILLETS AND PAT DRY. ARRANGE FISH IN SINGLE LAYER IN DISH. SPRINKLE WITH CHEESE AND TOP WITH TOMATO SLICES. SPRINKLE SEASONINGS OVER ALL. BAKE 15 MINUTES OR UNTIL OPAQUE AND FISH FLAKES. SERVE IMMEDIATELY WITH RICE, ASPARAGUS AND CRUNCHY CARROT STICKS.

TERIYAKI BAR-B-QUED SALMON STEAKS

4 TO 6 SALMON STEAKS	
1 CUP SOYA SAUCE	250 mL
2 TBSPS. BROWN SUGAR	30 mL
1 TBSP. DRY MUSTARD	15 mL

MIX SOYA SAUCE, BROWN SUGAR AND MUSTARD TOGETHER. MARINATE SALMON IN MIXTURE AT LEAST ONE HOUR BEFORE COOKING. BAR-B-QUE (OR BROIL) FOR 4 TO 5 MINUTES EACH SIDE, DEPENDING ON THICKNESS OF STEAKS. BRUSH MARINADE ON STEAKS AS THEY COOK. SERVES 4 TO 6. SERVE WITH RICE AND GREEN SALAD.

MARINATED FISH FILLETS WITH BASIL BUTTER

THE FISH IS MOIST, THE CALORIES ARE MINIMAL AND THE TASTE IS TERRIFIC! USE FRESH FISH AND FRESH HERBS IF AVAILABLE.

2	TBSPS. LIME JUICE	30 mL
2	TBSPS. OIL	30 mL
4	FISH FILLETS	500 g
1	TBSP. LEMON JUICE	15 mL
1	TBSP. BUTTER-MELTED	15 mL
1	TBSP. FRESH BASIL (OR DILL OR TARRAGON)	15 mL
	OR ½ TSP. DRIED BASIL, DILL OR TARRAGON	2 mL
	SALT & PEPPER TO TASTE	

WHISK TOGETHER LIME JUICE AND OIL. MARINATE FISH IN MIXTURE FOR 1 HOUR BEFORE COOKING. REMOVE FILLETS FROM MIXTURE AND ARRANGE IN A SINGLE LAYER IN A MICROWAVE OR CONVENTIONAL OVEN BAKING DISH. IN A SMALL DISH, MIX LEMON JUICE, BUTTER AND BASIL. DRIZZLE OVER FISH. SPRINKLE WITH SALT AND PEPPER. BAKE UNCOVERED AT 450° FOR 8 TO 10 MINUTES OR UNTIL FISH IS OPAQUE. SERVES 4. FOR MICROWAVE: COVER WITH PLASTIC WRAP; TURN BACK ONE CORNER TO VENT STEAM. MICROWAVE ON HIGH FOR 3½ TO 4 MINUTES.

POTLATCH SALMON

A WONDERFUL WAY TO COOK A WHOLE SALMON—
FAST AND EASY BAR-B-QUE.

1	WHOLE SALMON - BUTTERFLIED	
2	TBSPS. BUTTER - SOFTENED	30 mL
	JUICE OF ONE LEMON	
2	TSPS. DRY MUSTARD	10 mL
2/3 TO 1	CUP BROWN SUGAR	150 - 250 mL

TO BUTTERFLY SALMON: REMOVE HEAD, TAIL AND
FINS. RUN SHARP KNIFE DOWN BACKBONE UNTIL
SALMON OPENS FLAT. PLACE SKIN SIDE DOWN ON
SHEET OF FOIL. SPREAD BUTTER OVER FISH.
SPRINKLE LIBERALLY WITH LEMON JUICE AND
MUSTARD. COVER WITH 1/4" TO 1/2" OF BROWN SUGAR.

TO COOK: PLACE ON BAR-B-QUE, LOWER LID AND
COOK OVER LOW HEAT FOR 20 TO 30 MINUTES. SALMON
IS COOKED WHEN FLESH FLAKES. DON'T OVERCOOK!

THE BOTTOM LINE: DEE-LISHUS!! SERVES 6 TO 8.

TODAY, A GIRLS' GOT TO STAY ON HER TOES—
TO AVOID THE HEELS!

Mussels and Scallops in Cream

2½ LBS. MUSSELS (FRESH)	1 kg
¼ CUP BUTTER	50 mL
1 LARGE ONION - CHOPPED	
3 CLOVES GARLIC - MINCED	
JUICE OF ½ LEMON	
1½ CUPS DRY WHITE WINE	375 mL
1½ LBS. SCALLOPS	750 g
2 CUPS WHIPPING CREAM	500 mL
½ CUP FRESH PARSLEY - CHOPPED	125 mL
FRESHLY GROUND BLACK PEPPER	

WASH MUSSELS IN COLD WATER, REMOVE BEARDS (ONE SHOULD ALWAYS SHAVE FOR COMPANY) AND DISCARD ANY THAT ARE NOT TIGHTLY CLOSED. IN LARGE, HEAVY SAUCEPAN, SAUTÉ ONION IN BUTTER UNTIL TRANSPARENT. ADD GARLIC, LEMON JUICE AND WINE; BRING TO A BOIL. ADD MUSSELS, COVER, REDUCE HEAT AND STEAM FOR 2 TO 3 MINUTES. SHELLS WILL OPEN. ADD SCALLOPS, COVER AND COOK 2 TO 3 MINUTES LONGER. REMOVE FROM HEAT AND GRADUALLY ADD CREAM, STIRRING UNTIL WELL BLENDED. SIMMER ON MEDIUM HEAT BEFORE SERVING. LADLE INTO SHALLOW SOUP BOWLS. GARNISH WITH PARSLEY AND PEPPER. SERVES 6. SERVE WITH LOTS OF CRUSTY BREAD FOR DUNKING IN THE SAUCE. SEE COVER PICTURE.

SEAFOOD KABOBS

<u>No</u> FUSS GOURMET. SERVE WITH SALAD - LOW CAL
AND DELICIOUS!

½ LB. SCALLOPS *		250 g
¾ LB. RAW SHRIMP (TAILS ON)		375 g
1 CANTALOUPE MELON (30 BALLS)		
1 HONEYDEW MELON (30 BALLS)		
¼ CUP LEMON JUICE		50 mL
2 TBSPS. BUTTER - MELTED		30 mL
¼ CUP BRIE CHEESE (REMOVE SKIN)		50 mL
¼ CUP LIGHT CREAM		50 mL

ON SIX 8" SKEWERS, ALTERNATE SEAFOOD AND
MELON BALLS. MIX LEMON JUICE AND BUTTER. BROIL
KABOBS 10 MINUTES, TURNING AND BRUSHING
OCCASIONALLY WITH LEMON JUICE MIXTURE. (SEAFOOD
SHOULD BE OPAQUE.) IN A SMALL SAUCEPAN, MELT
CHEESE AND GRADUALLY WHISK IN CREAM. DRIZZLE THE
CHEESE MIXTURE OVER KABOBS. BROIL UNTIL GOLDEN
BROWN. SERVE OVER RICE. SERVES 6.
* NOTE: 2 LBS. OF FIRM FISH SUCH AS MONKFISH,
SHARK OR SWORDFISH IS A TASTY ALTERNATIVE TO
THE SCALLOPS AND SHRIMP.

WHAT YOU SEIZE IS WHAT YOU GET!

MY BAMBINO'S FAVOURITE!

1 LB. HOT ITALIAN SAUSAGE	500 g
1 LB. BEEF AND PORK SAUSAGE	500 g
¼ CUP VINEGAR	50 mL
4 CUPS WATER	1 L
1 - 28 OZ. CAN TOMATOES - MASHED	796 mL
1 - 14 OZ. CAN TOMATO SAUCE	398 mL
¾ CUP WATER	175 mL
1½ TSP. SALT	7 mL
1 CLOVE GARLIC	
2 TSPS. OREGANO	10 mL
1 TSP. BASIL	5 mL
1 TSP. THYME	5 mL
½ TSP. SAGE	2 mL
1½ TSPS. SUGAR	7 mL
½ TSP. WORCESTERSHIRE SAUCE	2 mL
SPAGHETTI - WHATEVER YOU THINK YOU NEED	

PLACE SAUSAGES IN LARGE FRYING PAN, ADDING VINEGAR AND WATER TO COVER. BOIL UNTIL ¾ REDUCED. DRAIN. RETURN SAUSAGE TO PAN AND LIGHTLY BROWN. REMOVE FROM PAN AND DRAIN ALL GREASE. CUT UP SAUSAGE. COMBINE ALL INGREDIENTS IN PAN. BRING TO BOIL AND SIMMER FOR 1 HOUR OR MORE. SERVE OVER COOKED SPAGHETTI. SERVES 6.

LINGUINI WITH RED CLAM SAUCE

1	MEDIUM ONION - CHOPPED	
3 TO 4	CLOVES GARLIC - MINCED	
3	STALKS CELERY - SLICED	
3	TBSPS. OLIVE OIL	45 mL
1 - 28 OZ.	CAN ITALIAN TOMATOES	796 mL
1	TSP. SALT	5 mL
2 - 7 OZ.	CANS BABY CLAMS - WITH LIQUID	2 - 198 mL
1	BAY LEAF	
1	TSP. DRIED OREGANO	5 mL
8	SLICES BACON - COOKED & CRUMBLED	
	COARSELY GROUND BLACK PEPPER TO TASTE	
	LINGUINI FOR FOUR PEOPLE	

IN MEDIUM SKILLET SAUTÉ ONION, GARLIC AND CELERY IN OIL UNTIL LIGHTLY GOLDEN. ADD NEXT 7 INGREDIENTS AND SIMMER, COVERED, FOR 1 HOUR OR MORE. JUST BEFORE SERVING, COOK LINGUINI. DRAIN WELL. MIX WITH HALF THE CLAM SAUCE AND TOSS. SERVE IN SHALLOW SOUP BOWLS. PASS THE REMAINING SAUCE.

WHY DO BANKS SAY WE SHOULD TRUST THEM WHEN THEY TURN AROUND AND CHAIN DOWN THE PENS.

PASTA WITH CRAB AND BASIL

WE'VE TRIED THIS WITH FRESH CRAB AND MOCK CRAB. BOTH WERE GREAT BUT THE LATTER IS FAR MORE REASONABLE.

¼	LB. BUTTER	125 g
2	TBSPS. SHALLOTS – CHOPPED	30 mL
2	TBSPS. FRESH BASIL – MINCED...OR...	30 mL
1	TSP. DRIED BASIL	5 mL
2	TBSPS. FRESH PARSLEY – MINCED	30 mL
3 – 14 OZ.	CANS TOMATOES – PEELED, CHOPPED AND DRAINED	3-398 mL
½	CUP DRY WHITE WINE	125 mL
1½	LBS. CRABMEAT OR MOCK CRAB	750 g
1	LB. VERMICELLI OR ANY FINE PASTA, COOKED AL DENTE AND DRAINED	500 g
	PARMESAN CHEESE – FRESHLY GRATED	

IN LARGE SKILLET, MELT BUTTER AND SAUTÉ SHALLOTS, BASIL AND PARSLEY FOR 2 TO 3 MINUTES. STIR IN TOMATOES AND HEAT TO BOILING. COOK UNTIL REDUCED BY HALF. ADD WINE AND SIMMER 5 MINUTES. ADD CRAB AND SIMMER 2 TO 3 MINUTES. SERVE OVER PASTA. SPRINKLE WITH PARMESAN. SERVES 6. PICTURED ON PAGE 69.

ONE WAY TO SAVE FACE IS TO KEEP THE LOWER HALF SHUT.

GOURMET MACARONI AND CHEESE

2½	CUPS MACARONI	625 mL
4	TBSPS. BUTTER	60 mL
4	TBSPS. FLOUR	60 mL
2	CUPS MILK	500 mL
1	TSP. SALT	5 mL
1	TSP. SUGAR	5 mL
½	LB. PROCESSED CHEESE - CUBED (VELVEETA)	250 g
⅔	CUP SOUR CREAM	150 mL
1⅓	CUPS COTTAGE CHEESE	325 mL
2	CUPS OLD CHEDDAR CHEESE - GRATED	500 mL
1½	CUPS SOFT BREADCRUMBS	375 mL
2	TBSPS. BUTTER	30 mL
	PAPRIKA	

COOK AND DRAIN MACARONI AND PLACE IN A 2½ QT. GREASED CASSEROLE. MELT BUTTER OVER MEDIUM HEAT, STIR IN FLOUR; MIX WELL. ADD MILK AND COOK OVER MEDIUM HEAT, STIRRING CONSTANTLY UNTIL SAUCE THICKENS. ADD SALT, SUGAR AND CHEESE. MIX WELL. MIX SOUR CREAM AND COTTAGE CHEESE INTO SAUCE. POUR OVER MACARONI. MIX WELL. SPRINKLE CHEDDAR CHEESE AND CRUMBS OVER TOP. DOT WITH BUTTER AND SPRINKLE WITH PAPRIKA. MAY BE FROZEN AT THIS POINT. BAKE AT 350° FOR 45 TO 50 MINUTES. SERVES 6.

WHEN YOU'RE OVER THE HILL - YOU PICK UP SPEED!

BÉCHAMEL SAUCE —

4 TBSPS. BUTTER	60 mL
3 TBSPS. FLOUR	45 mL
2 CUPS MILK – HEATED	500 mL
SALT & PEPPER TO TASTE	

½ CUP MINCED ONION	125 mL
¼ CUP OIL	50 mL
2 MEDIUM TOMATOES - PEELED, SEEDED & CHOPPED	
3 TBSPS. FRESH PARSLEY – CHOPPED	45 mL
3 CUPS FRESH MUSHROOMS – SLICED	750 g
SALT & PEPPER TO TASTE	

12 LASAGNA NOODLES	
2 CUPS BÉCHAMEL SAUCE	500 mL
1½ LBS. HAM-CUT INTO THIN STRIPS	750 g
⅔ CUP PARMESAN CHEESE - GRATED	150 mL
4 TBSPS. BUTTER	60 mL

TO MAKE BÉCHAMEL SAUCE, MELT BUTTER IN A SAUCEPAN. ADD THE FLOUR AND STIR UNTIL SMOOTH, 3 OR 4 MINUTES. SLOWLY ADD THE MILK, STIRRING CONSTANTLY. SEASON WITH SALT AND PEPPER. CONTINUE COOKING OVER LOW HEAT UNTIL THICKENED. COVER AND SET ASIDE.

THERE'S MORE – SEE PAGE 137

HAM AND MUSHROOM LASAGNA

THIS RECIPE CONTINUED FROM PAGE 136.

SAUTÉ ONION IN OIL. ADD TOMATOES AND PARSLEY. COOK OVER MODERATE HEAT UNTIL LIQUID HAS EVAPORATED. ADD THE MUSHROOMS, SALT AND PEPPER; MIX WELL, SET ASIDE. PREHEAT OVEN TO 350°. COOK NOODLES ACCORDING TO PACKAGE DIRECTIONS. DRAIN. BUTTER A 9"×13" DISH. PLACE A LAYER OF NOODLES IN THE BOTTOM OF THE DISH, FOLLOWED BY A LAYER OF HALF THE MUSHROOM MIXTURE. NEXT, DRIZZLE ½ CUP BÉCHAMEL SAUCE AND THEN ADD A LAYER OF HAM AND SPRINKLE WITH PARMESAN CHEESE. REPEAT THE LAYERS AND TOP WITH A LAYER OF NOODLES. POUR THE REMAINING 1 CUP OF BÉCHAMEL SAUCE ON TOP AND DOT WITH BUTTER. BAKE UNCOVERED 25 TO 30 MINUTES OR UNTIL HOT AND BUBBLY. SERVES 6 TO 8. IF FROZEN, PREPARE 1 CUP BÉCHAMEL SAUCE AND POUR OVER LASAGNA BEFORE HEATING.

TO GET MAXIMUM ATTENTION, IT'S HARD TO BEAT A GOOD, BIG MISTAKE!

PASTA PRIMAVERA

RAID THE GARDEN AND GET OUT THE VINO—
IT'S ITALIAN TONIGHT!

1	BUNCH BROCCOLI - FLOWERETTES ONLY	
1	BUNCH ASPARAGUS - TIPS ONLY	
1	SMALL ZUCCHINI - SLICED	
1	CUP GREEN BEANS - CUT	250 mL
1/2	CUP PEAS	125 mL
2	TBSPS. BUTTER	30 mL
1	CUP MUSHROOMS - THINLY SLICED	250 mL
1	BUNCH GREEN ONIONS - CHOPPED	
2	CLOVES GARLIC - MINCED	
2	CUPS CHERRY TOMATOES - CUT IN HALVES	500 mL
1/4	CUP PARSLEY - CHOPPED	50 mL
2	TBSPS. FRESH BASIL - CHOPPED (1 TSP. DRIED)	30 mL
1/2	TSP. DRIED RED PEPPER FLAKES	2 mL
1/4	CUP BUTTER	50 mL
2	TBSPS. CHICKEN BROTH	30 mL
3/4	CUP HEAVY CREAM	175 mL
2/3	CUP PARMESAN CHEESE - GRATED	150 mL
	SALT AND FRESHLY GROUND PEPPER TO TASTE	
	TOASTED PINE NUTS (OPTIONAL)	
1	LB. VERMICELLI - COOKED 'AL DENTE'	500 g

COOK FIRST FIVE VEGETABLES IN BOILING WATER
UNTIL TENDER CRISP. RINSE IMMEDIATELY IN COLD WATER
UNTIL CHILLED. DRAIN WELL. (HOT TIP FROM MOMMA LEONE—
"YOU KEEP THE VEGETABLES CRISP") — CONTINUED - PAGE 141.

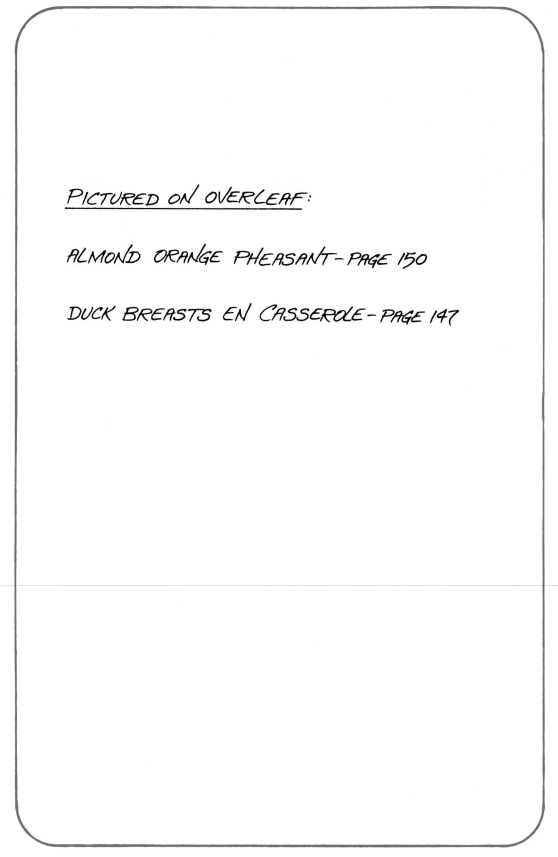

PICTURED ON OVERLEAF:

ALMOND ORANGE PHEASANT – PAGE 150

DUCK BREASTS EN CASSEROLE – PAGE 147

PASTA PRIMAVERA

THIS RECIPE CONTINUED FROM PAGE 138.

IN A MEDIUM-SIZED SKILLET SAUTÉ MUSHROOMS, ONIONS AND GARLIC IN 2 TBSPS. OF BUTTER FOR 2 TO 3 MINUTES. ADD TOMATOES AND COOK 1 MINUTE MORE, STIRRING GENTLY. ADD TO THE VEGETABLES ALONG WITH PARSLEY, BASIL AND RED PEPPER FLAKES. IN A LARGE POT, MELT 1/4 CUP BUTTER. ADD CHICKEN BROTH, CREAM, CHEESE AND SALT AND PEPPER. STIR WITH A WHISK UNTIL SMOOTH BUT DO NOT BOIL. ADD VEGETABLES AND HEAT THROUGH. CHECK SEASONING. SERVE IMMEDIATELY ON COOKED PASTA. SPRINKLE WITH TOASTED PINE NUTS.

A VIRGIN FOREST IS A PLACE WHERE THE HAND OF MAN HAS NEVER SET FOOT.

EASY AND GOOD!

3 TO 4 TBSPS. OLIVE OIL	45 - 60 mL
4 CLOVES GARLIC - MINCED	
1/2 TSP. RED PEPPER FLAKES - HOT	2 mL
1 - 28 oz. CAN ITALIAN TOMATOES (PURÉED)	796 mL
1 TSP. SALT	5 mL
1/2 TSP. FRESHLY GROUND PEPPER	2 mL
1/4 CUP FRESH PARSLEY - CHOPPED	50 mL
1/2 CUP FRESHLY GRATED PARMESAN CHEESE	125 mL
1 LB. PENNE NOODLES	500 g

IN A LARGE HEAVY FRYING PAN, HEAT OIL; ADD GARLIC AND PEPPER FLAKES. DO NOT BROWN. STIR IN TOMATOES, SALT AND PEPPER. COOK FOR 10 TO 15 MINUTES OR UNTIL THICKENED. STIR IN HALF OF THE PARSLEY. SET ASIDE. IN A LARGE POT OF BOILING, SALTED WATER, COOK PENNE FOR 10 TO 15 MINUTES. DRAIN WELL. PUT IN SERVING BOWL OR PLATTER. REHEAT SAUCE AND POUR OVER PENNE. SPRINKLE WITH PARMESAN AND REMAINING PARSLEY. TOSS WELL AND SERVE 6.

I'M NOT YOUNG ENOUGH TO KNOW EVERYTHING.

8 LASAGNA NOODLES	
1/2 CUP ONION-CHOPPED	125 mL
2 TO 4 CLOVES GARLIC-CRUSHED	
3 TBSPS. BUTTER	45 mL
2 TBSPS. CORNSTARCH	30 mL
2 TBSPS. PARSLEY	30 mL
1 TSP. BASIL	5 mL
1/8 TSP. NUTMEG	.5 mL
2 CUPS MILK	500 mL
1 - 10 OZ. PKG. FROZEN CHOPPED SPINACH— THAWED & DRAINED	300 g
1/2 CUP RIPE OLIVES-SLICED	125 mL
2 CUPS RICOTTA OR COTTAGE CHEESE	500 mL
1 EGG - BEATEN	
1 CUP MOZZARELLA CHEESE - GRATED	250 mL
1/2 CUP GRATED PARMESAN CHEESE	125 mL

COOK LASAGNA NOODLES UNTIL TENDER - DRAIN AND RINSE IN COLD WATER. IN MEDIUM SAUCEPAN, SAUTÉ ONION AND GARLIC IN BUTTER. STIR IN CORNSTARCH, PARSLEY, BASIL, NUTMEG AND MILK. COOK UNTIL THICKENED. ADD SPINACH AND OLIVES. SET ASIDE. IN MEDIUM BOWL MIX RICOTTA CHEESE, EGG, MOZZARELLA CHEESE AND 1/4 CUP PARMESAN CHEESE. SET ASIDE. ARRANGE 4 LASAGNA NOODLES IN BOTTOM OF 9"x 13" PAN. TOP WITH HALF SPINACH MIXTURE, THEN HALF CHEESE MIXTURE. REPEAT LAYERS. SPRINKLE WITH REMAINING PARMESAN CHEESE. BAKE 350° - 45 MINUTES.

SPAGHETTI CARBONARA

2	TBSPS. OLIVE OIL	30 mL
1	TSP. GARLIC - MINCED	5 mL
8	THIN SLICES PROSCIUTTO - CHOPPED	
	(BACON OR HAM MAY BE USED).	
5	EGG YOLKS	
1	LB. SPAGHETTI	500 g
½	CUP CREAM	125 mL
½	CUP PARMESAN CHEESE	125 mL
	FRESHLY GROUND PEPPER TO TASTE	

SAUTÉ GARLIC AND HAM IN OLIVE OIL. BEAT YOLKS. COOK SPAGHETTI; DRAIN AND RETURN TO POT TO KEEP WARM. ADD HAM MIXTURE AND YOLKS TO SPAGHETTI AND TOSS THOROUGHLY. ADD CREAM AND PARMESAN. COMBINE WELL AND HEAT THROUGH. SERVE IMMEDIATELY AND PASS THE PEPPER MILL! SERVES 6.

THERE'S ONE GOOD THING ABOUT A DENTIST APPOINTMENT. YOU DON'T HAVE TO GET WEIGHED FIRST.

Broccoli Lasagna au Gratin

9	LASAGNA NOODLES – COOKED	
2	PKGS. FROZEN CHOPPED BROCCOLI –	
	DRAINED & THAWED	2-300 g
2	CUPS COTTAGE CHEESE	500 mL
2	EGGS – SLIGHTLY BEATEN	
1	– 24 oz. JAR SPICY SPAGHETTI SAUCE	750 mL
2	CUPS MOZZARELLA CHEESE – SHREDDED	500 mL
½	CUP PARMESAN CHEESE – GRATED	125 mL

SPREAD A THIN LAYER OF SPAGHETTI SAUCE IN A 9" x 13" PAN. COVER WITH 3 LASAGNA NOODLES. MIX BROCCOLI, COTTAGE CHEESE AND EGGS TOGETHER. SPREAD ⅓ OF MIXTURE OVER NOODLES. TOP WITH A ⅓ OF REMAINING SPAGHETTI SAUCE, ⅓ MOZZARELLA AND ⅓ PARMESAN. REPEAT LAYERING TWICE. BAKE AT 350° FOR 30 TO 35 MINUTES. SERVES 8 TO 10.

SURE THE COST OF LIVING IS HIGH –
BUT CONSIDER THE ALTERNATIVE!

CRISPY SESAME CHICKEN

FORGET SHAKE 'N BAKE —
TRY THIS!

3 LBS. CUT UP CHICKEN		1.5 kg
MAYONNAISE		
1 CUP CORNFLAKES OR HONEYNUT CORNFLAKES-		
CRUSHED		250 mL
2 TBSPS. SESAME SEEDS		30 mL
SALT & PEPPER TO TASTE		

COAT CHICKEN WITH MAYONNAISE. MIX CORNFLAKES, SESAME SEEDS, SALT AND PEPPER TOGETHER IN A SHALLOW DISH. ROLL CHICKEN IN MIXTURE UNTIL PIECES ARE WELL COATED. PLACE IN OVEN-PROOF DISH AND BAKE AT 350° FOR 1 TO 1½ HOURS. SERVES 6.

A VERBAL CONTRACT ISN'T WORTH THE
PAPER IT'S WRITTEN ON.

DUCK BREASTS EN CASSEROLE

A PLEASANT CHANGE FROM THE TRADITIONAL ROAST DUCK. SEE PICTURE, PAGE 139.

3	LARGE DUCK BREASTS	
1/4	CUP FLOUR	50 mL
1 1/2	TSPS. SALT	7 mL
2	TSPS. PAPRIKA	10 mL
1/4	CUP BUTTER - MELTED	50 mL
1 - 10 oz.	CAN WHOLE MUSHROOMS - DRAINED,	284 mL
	(RESERVE LIQUID)	
2	BEEF BOUILLON CUBES	
1 - 14 oz.	CAN TOMATO SAUCE	398 mL
1/2	CUP GREEN PEPPER - CHOPPED	125 mL
1/4	CUP CELERY - CHOPPED	50 mL
1/4	CUP ONION - CHOPPED	50 mL
	DRY RED WINE - MAYBE	

CUT BREAST HALVES INTO 8 PIECES. SHAKE IN A BAG WITH FLOUR, SALT AND PAPRIKA. USE ALL THE FLOUR MIXTURE OR SAUCE WILL BE THIN. BROWN BREASTS IN BUTTER. PLACE IN CASSEROLE. DISSOLVE BOUILLON CUBES IN 2 CUPS HOT WATER PLUS MUSHROOM LIQUID. POUR OVER DUCK. ADD SCRAPINGS FROM BROWNING PAN. BAKE AT 300° FOR 1 HOUR. BLEND TOMATO SAUCE, GREEN PEPPER, CELERY, ONIONS AND MUSHROOMS. ADD TO THE CASSEROLE AND STIR WELL. BAKE ANOTHER HOUR OR MORE, STIRRING OCCASIONALLY. ADD MORE LIQUID IF NECESSARY - HERE IT COMES - DRY RED WINE IS BEST. SERVES 6.

SWEET AND SPICY CASHEW CHICKEN

A DELICIOUS AND COLOURFUL CHINESE DISH. SERVE OVER RICE ON A LARGE PLATTER. OR TAKE WOK RIGHT TO THE TABLE. SEE PICTURE, PAGE 103.

SAUCE —

½	CUP KETCHUP	125 mL
4	TSPS. SOYA SAUCE	20 mL
½	TSP. SALT	2 mL
2	TBSPS. WORCESTERSHIRE SAUCE	30 mL
3	TBSPS. SUGAR	45 mL
1½	TSPS. SESAME OIL (ORIENTAL)	7 mL
¼	TSP. CAYENNE PEPPER	1 mL
½	CUP CHICKEN BROTH	125 mL

THE REST:

2	TBSPS. CORNSTARCH	30 mL
½	TSP. SUGAR	2 mL
¼	TSP. SALT	1 mL
3	WHOLE BONELESS CHICKEN BREASTS — SKINNED & CUT INTO ¾" CUBES	
¼	CUP OIL	50 mL
2 TO 3	TBSPS. MINCED FRESH GINGEROOT	30-45 mL
1	TBSP. MINCED GARLIC	15 mL
1	SMALL ONION - CHOPPED	
2	RED BELL PEPPERS - CUT INTO 1" TRIANGLES	
2	CARROTS - SLICED DIAGONALLY AND THINLY	
2	CUPS SNOW PEAS	500 mL
1½	CUPS CASHEWS	375 mL

THAT'S WHAT YOU NEED - METHOD NEXT PAGE.

SWEET AND SPICY CASHEW CHICKEN

THIS RECIPE CONTINUED FROM PAGE 148.

COMBINE SAUCE INGREDIENTS AND SET ASIDE. IN A BOWL, COMBINE CORNSTARCH, SUGAR AND SALT. ADD CHICKEN AND TOSS. HEAT WOK OR FRYING PAN TO HIGHEST HEAT. ADD OIL. HEAT TO HOT, NOT SMOKING. ADD CHICKEN, GINGER, GARLIC AND ONION. STIR UNTIL CHICKEN IS OPAQUE (ABOUT ONE MINUTE). ADD PEPPERS AND CARROTS. STIR 2 TO 3 MINUTES. ADD PEAS AND SAUCE. COOK UNTIL IT COMES TO A BOIL. ADD CASHEWS AND SERVE IMMEDIATELY. SERVES 6.

CHICKEN PARMESAN

GEPPETTO'S FAVOURITE.

2	WHOLE CHICKEN BREASTS - HALVED AND BONED	
3	EGGS - BEATEN	
1	CUP BREAD CRUMBS	250 mL
3	TBSPS. PARMESAN CHEESE - GRATED	45 mL
1 - 14 oz.	CAN TOMATO SAUCE	398 mL
½	CUP MOZZARELLA CHEESE - GRATED	125 mL
¼	CUP PARMESAN CHEESE - GRATED	50 mL

MIX BREAD CRUMBS AND 3 TBSPS. PARMESAN CHEESE TOGETHER. DIP CHICKEN PIECES IN EGGS, THEN IN CRUMB MIXTURE. FRY UNTIL GOLDEN BROWN. PUT PIECES IN BAKING DISH AND SPREAD TOMATO SAUCE OVER ALL. SPRINKLE WITH MOZZARELLA AND PARMESAN CHEESES. BAKE AT 350° FOR 1 HOUR. SERVES 4.

ALMOND ORANGE PHEASANT
(OR CORNISH HENS)

SEE PICTURE, PAGE 139.

1 WILD PHEASANT <u>OR</u> 2 CORNISH HENS	
THE MARINADE —	
½ TSP. TARRAGON	2 mL
½ TSP. POULTRY SEASONING	2 mL
½ TSP. PEPPER	2 mL
1 TSP. GINGER	5 mL
2 TSPS. SALT	10 mL
2 TSPS. GRATED ORANGE RIND	10 mL
3 TBSPS. OIL	45 mL
2 TBSPS. LIQUID HONEY	30 mL
¼ CUP GREEN ONION — CHOPPED	50 mL
¼ CUP CELERY — FINELY CHOPPED	50 mL
¼ CUP VINEGAR	50 mL
2 TBSPS. LIME JUICE	30 mL
1 CUP DRY WHITE WINE (ADD AN EXTRA GLASS FOR THE COOK)	250 mL
1 - 10 OZ. CAN MANDARIN ORANGE SEGMENTS	284 mL
1 CUP JUICE FROM CANNED ORANGES (ADD ENOUGH WATER TO MAKE ONE CUP)	250 mL
THE DRESSING —	
⅓ CUP WILD OR WHITE RICE	75 mL
STRAINED FRUIT & VEGETABLE MIXTURE	
¼ CUP ALMONDS — SLIVERED & TOASTED	50 mL
THE GARNISH —	
1 - 10 OZ. CAN MANDARIN ORANGE SEGMENTS	284 mL
PARSLEY	SOME

ALMOND ORANGE PHEASANT
(OR CORNISH HENS)

THIS RECIPE CONTINUED FROM PAGE 150.

COMBINE MARINADE INGREDIENTS IN MEDIUM-SIZED MIXING BOWL (NOT METAL). PLACE PHEASANT OR TWO CORNISH GAME HENS IN MARINADE, COVER AND REFRIGERATE OVERNIGHT. COOK RICE. REMOVE BIRDS FROM MARINADE. STRAIN MARINADE INTO SMALL BOWL, RESERVING FRUIT AND VEGETABLES FOR DRESSING. TO MAKE DRESSING, COMBINE RICE, FRUIT, VEGETABLES AND ALMONDS. STUFF BIRD, SKEWER CAVITY CLOSED AND TIE LEGS TOGETHER. PLACE IN SMALL ROASTING PAN, POUR RESERVED MARINADE OVER BIRD, COVER AND ROAST AT 375° FOR 1 HOUR OR UNTIL LEGS ARE TENDER. REMOVE COVER, BASTE AND INCREASE TEMPERATURE TO 400°. COOK 5 MORE MINUTES OR UNTIL GOLDEN. PLACE BIRD ON PLATTER. ADD 2 TBSPS. CORNSTARCH DISSOLVED IN 1/4 CUP OF COLD WATER TO REMAINING JUICES AND COOK UNTIL THICKENED. GARNISH WITH PARSLEY AND MANDARIN ORANGE SLICES. MAKE "SOCKS" FOR THE PHEASANT OUT OF A BROWN PAPER BAG (THEY'RE OVER DRESSED IN WHITE!). YOU'VE DONE IT AGAIN, YOU CLEVER GOURMET! SERVES 2 - YOU DIDN'T WANT COMPANY ANYWAY.

THE TROUBLE WITH THE RAT RACE IS THAT EVEN IF YOU WIN, YOU'RE STILL A RAT.

CHICKEN CATCH-A-TORY

EVEN LIBERALS ARE WON OVER BY THIS ONE!

3	WHOLE CHICKEN BREASTS - SKINNED, BONED AND CUT INTO PIECES	
	FLOUR	
	OIL	
1 - 28 oz.	CAN TOMATOES	796 mL
½	CUP WHITE WINE	125 mL
2	TBSPS. ONION - MINCED	30 mL
⅛	TSP. GARLIC POWDER	½ mL
⅛	TSP. ALLSPICE	½ mL
¼	TSP. BLACK PEPPER	1 mL
1	TSP. ITALIAN SEASONING	5 mL
¼	TSP. PAPRIKA	1 mL
1	TSP. OREGANO	5 mL
2	TSPS. SEASONED SALT	10 mL

DREDGE CHICKEN IN FLOUR AND FRY IN OIL AT HIGH HEAT UNTIL GOLDEN (ABOUT 3 MINUTES). DRAIN OFF OIL. ADD REMAINING INGREDIENTS TO CHICKEN AND SIMMER 45 MINUTES. SERVE OVER SPAGHETTI OR WITH RICE - TO A CAUCUS OF 6.

LEAD ME NOT INTO TEMPTATION -
I CAN FIND IT BY MYSELF.

CHICKEN ENCHILADA CASSEROLE

THIS IS A MUST TO TRY!

3 TO 4 CUPS CHICKEN-COOKED AND CUT INTO LARGE BITE-SIZED PIECES	1 kg
6 SMALL CORN OR FLOUR TORTILLAS (OR 3 LARGE)	
1 LARGE ONION -DICED	
2 TBSPS. OIL	30 mL
1- 4 OZ. CAN GREEN CHILIES-SEEDED & FINELY CHOPPED	115 g
1-10 OZ. CAN CREAM OF MUSHROOM SOUP	284 mL
2 CUPS CHEDDAR CHEESE - GRATED	500 mL
2 CUPS MOZZARELLA CHEESE - GRATED	500 mL
1 CUP SALSA	250 mL

CUT TORTILLAS INTO 6 PIECES EACH. SAUTÉ ONION IN OIL. ADD CHILIES, SOUP AND HALF THE GRATED CHEESES. COOK SLOWLY UNTIL CHEESE MELTS. LINE A BUTTERED 1½ QT. CASSEROLE WITH HALF THE TORTILLA PIECES. COVER WITH ½ CUP SALSA. LAYER WITH HALF THE CHICKEN, THEN HALF THE CHEESE SAUCE. REPEAT LAYERS. TOP WITH THE REMAINING GRATED CHEESES. BAKE AT 325° FOR 50 TO 60 MINUTES. LET STAND (OR SIT IF YOU PREFER!) FOR 10 MINUTES. SERVES 6.

A MAN IN LOVE IS INCOMPLETE UNTIL HE'S MARRIED - THEN HE'S FINISHED!

3	WHOLE CHICKEN BREASTS-SKINNED & BONED	
4	TBSPS. FLOUR	60 mL
5	TBSPS. OIL	75 mL
2	TSPS. POWDERED CHICKEN BOUILLON....	10 mL
	DISSOLVED IN:	
½	CUP WATER	125 mL
1	TBSP. BROWN SUGAR	15 mL
2 TO 3	TSPS. CURRY POWDER	10-15 mL
½	TSP. SALT	2 mL
2	TBSPS. LEMON JUICE	30 mL
2	TBSPS. SOYA SAUCE	30 mL
2	TBSPS. CORNSTARCH - DISSOLVED IN:	30 mL
¼	CUP WATER	50 mL
1	MEDIUM ONION - CHOPPED	
1	- 8 OZ. CAN WATER CHESTNUTS - DRAINED	227 mL
1	-10 OZ. CAN APRICOTS - WITH JUICE	284 mL

CUT CHICKEN INTO LARGE PIECES, SHAKE IN FLOUR & BROWN IN OIL. SET IN 2½ QT. CASSEROLE DISH. IN A BOWL, COMBINE REMAINING INGREDIENTS. POUR OVER CHICKEN, COVER AND COOK AT 350° FOR 1 HOUR. SERVES 6.

SOME COME TO THE 'FOUNTAIN OF KNOWLEDGE' TO DRINK... I PREFER TO JUST GARGLE.

THANKS FOR THE MEMORIES!

PASTRY TO COVER 3 QT. CASSEROLE OR
    FROZEN PUFF PASTRY DOUGH

½	CUP BUTTER OR MARGARINE	125 mL
½	CUP FLOUR	125 mL
1	TSP. SALT	5 mL
	PEPPER TO TASTE	
2	TBSPS. ONION - FINELY CHOPPED	30 mL
3	CUPS CHICKEN BROTH	750 mL
½	LB. MUSHROOMS - SLICED	250 g
3	TBSPS. BUTTER OR MARGARINE	45 mL
3	CUPS CHICKEN - COOKED & DICED	750 mL
2	CARROTS - FINELY CHOPPED	
2	STALKS CELERY - FINELY CHOPPED	
2	POTATOES - CUBED	

MELT BUTTER IN SAUCEPAN OVER MEDIUM HEAT. BLEND IN FLOUR, SALT, PEPPER AND ONION. GRADUALLY STIR IN CHICKEN BROTH. COOK, STIRRING CONSTANTLY UNTIL SMOOTH AND THICKENED. IN A SMALL FRY PAN, COOK THE MUSHROOMS IN BUTTER. ADD MUSHROOMS, CHICKEN, CARROTS, CELERY AND POTATOES TO SAUCE. MIX WELL AND POUR INTO LARGE CASSEROLE. COVER WITH PASTRY AND SLASH (WATCH IT) TO ALLOW STEAM TO ESCAPE. BAKE IN PREHEATED 400° OVEN FOR ABOUT 30 MINUTES OR UNTIL PASTRY IS GOLDEN AND CHICKEN MIXTURE BUBBLY.

WHIP-LASH CHICKEN

HOT AND SPICY - OOH-DA-LOLLY!

1	LARGE ONION - THINLY SLICED & SEPARATED INTO RINGS	
1	GREEN PEPPER - CUT INTO THIN STRIPS	
1	CUP MUSHROOMS - SLICED	250 mL
2	TBSPS. WATER	30 mL
2	TSPS. OREGANO	10 mL
2	TSPS. CRUSHED RED PEPPER (HOT!)	10 mL
1	TSP. GARLIC SALT	5 mL
½	TSP. HOT PEPPER SAUCE	2 mL
1 - 14 oz.	CAN TOMATOES	398 mL
⅔	CUP PEANUT BUTTER	150 mL
2	TSPS. INSTANT CHICKEN BOUILLON	10 mL
3	WHOLE CHICKEN BREASTS - SKINNED, BONED AND CUT INTO BITE-SIZED PIECES.	

IN A LARGE SAUCEPAN, COMBINE ONION, GREEN PEPPER, MUSHROOM, WATER, OREGANO, RED PEPPER, GARLIC SALT AND HOT PEPPER SAUCE. COOK OVER MEDIUM HEAT, STIRRING FREQUENTLY UNTIL VEGGIES ARE TENDER CRISP. IN A BLENDER OR FOOD PROCESSOR, COMBINE UNDRAINED TOMATOES, PEANUT BUTTER AND BOUILLON. PROCESS TIL SMOOTH. PLACE UNCOOKED CHICKEN IN A LARGE CASSEROLE. TOP WITH VEGGIE MIXTURE. POUR TOMATO MIXTURE OVER ALL. COVER AND BAKE AT 350° FOR 50 MINUTES. SERVE WITH RICE TO 8 FOLKS.

PICTURED ON OVERLEAF:

HAZELNUT TORTE - PAGE 194

LEMON SORBET - PAGE 190

SHORTBREAD TARTS WITH CHEESE 'N' FRUIT —
PAGE 178

CHICKEN MEXICANA

CHA, CHA, CHA!

4	LBS. CHICKEN BREASTS	2 kg
3	CUPS WATER	750 mL
1	TSP. SALT	5 mL
2	TBSPS. BUTTER	30 mL
1	MEDIUM ONION - FINELY CHOPPED	
1	GREEN PEPPER - SEEDED & CHOPPED	
2	CLOVES GARLIC - CRUSHED	
1- 28 oz.	CAN TOMATOES	796 mL
2-10 oz.	CANS BUTTON MUSHROOMS	2-284 mL
4	TBSPS. PARSLEY	60 mL
1	TSP. SUGAR	5 mL
1	TSP. PEPPER	5 mL
1	TSP. CHILI POWDER	5 mL
½	TSP. OREGANO	2 mL
1	TBSP. CORNSTARCH	15 mL
2	TBSPS. COLD WATER	30 mL

SIMMER CHICKEN IN WATER AND SALT FOR ½ HOUR.
DISCARD BONES AND SKIN. CUT CHICKEN INTO LARGE PIECES
AND SET ASIDE. SAVE 2 CUPS OF BROTH. SAUTÉ ONION, GREEN
PEPPER AND GARLIC IN BUTTER. COMBINE TOMATOES,
MUSHROOMS, PARSLEY, SUGAR, PEPPER, CHILI POWDER AND
OREGANO, THEN ADD TO SAUTÉED MIXTURE. ADD RESERVED
BROTH. MIX CORNSTARCH WITH WATER AND ADD TO SAUCE
MIXTURE. COOK FOR 1 MINUTE. PUT CHICKEN PIECES IN LARGE
CASSEROLE; POUR SAUCE OVER. HEAT, COVERED AT 400°
FOR 30 MINUTES BEFORE SERVING. SERVES 10 TO 12.

SERVE THIS TO YOUR FAMILY WITH RICE AND STIR-FRIED BROCCOLI OR ASPARAGUS (PORK IN MUSHROOM SOUP _DOES_ GET TEDIOUS!) SERVES 6.

12 BONELESS PORK CHOPS - FAT REMOVED		
1/4 CUP MILK	50 mL	
1/4 CUP FINE BREADCRUMBS	50 mL	
1/4 CUP FLOUR	50 mL	
SALT & PEPPER TO TASTE		
1/4 CUP OIL	50 mL	
SAUCE :		
1 MEDIUM ONION		
1 TBSP. OIL	15 mL	
1 TBSP. CORNSTARCH	15 mL	
1/4 CUP COLD WATER	50 mL	
1 - 14 oz. CAN TOMATOES - QUARTERED, WITH JUICE	398 mL	
2 TBSPS. KETCHUP	30 mL	
1 TBSP. H.P. SAUCE	15 mL	
1 TO 2 TBSP. HONEY _OR_ BROWN SUGAR	15-30 mL	

DIP CHOPS INTO MILK, THEN INTO MIXTURE OF BREADCRUMBS, FLOUR, SALT AND PEPPER. FRY IN OIL OVER MEDIUM HEAT UNTIL CHOPS ARE BROWNED. DRAIN AND SET IN SHALLOW CASSEROLE. TO MAKE SAUCE, CUT ONION IN HALF LENGTHWISE AND SLICE FINELY TO FORM HALF RINGS. BROWN IN OIL. COMBINE CORNSTARCH AND COLD WATER. ADD TOMATOES, CORNSTARCH MIXTURE AND REMAINING INGREDIENTS AND BRING TO BOIL. POUR OVER PORK, COVER AND BAKE AT 300° FOR 30 MINUTES.

Holy Ham Loaf
with Marvelous Mustard Sauce

This is the dinner we always look forward to when visiting Grandma!

1/3 cup Brown Sugar	75 mL
1 - 14 oz. can crushed Pineapple - well drained	398 mL
1 lb. lean Ground Ham (lean cottage roll)	500 g
1 lb. lean Ground Pork	500 g
1 cup Bread Crumbs	250 mL
1/4 tsp. Pepper	1 mL
2 Eggs - Beaten	
1 cup Milk	250 mL

The Sauce:

1 cup Brown Sugar	250 mL
2 tbsps. Dry Mustard	30 mL
2/3 cup Vinegar	150 mL
2 Eggs - well beaten	

Line a loaf pan with foil. Mix brown sugar and pineapple together and pour into pan. Combine ham, pork, bread crumbs, pepper, eggs and milk. Press down on pineapple. Bake at 375° for 1 1/4 hours. While loaf is baking, combine ingredients for sauce. Cook slowly until thickened. Invert ham loaf onto platter and serve with mustard sauce. Freezes well - serves six.

MICROWAVE PEANUT BRITTLE

GREAT FOR GIFTS!

1 CUP RAW PEANUTS, PECANS OR CASHEWS	250 mL
1 CUP SUGAR	250 mL
½ CUP CORN SYRUP	125 mL
PINCH SALT	
1 TSP. BUTTER	5 mL
1 TSP. VANILLA	5 mL
1 TSP. BAKING SODA	5 mL

STIR FIRST FOUR INGREDIENTS TOGETHER IN AN
8 CUP MEASURING CUP, OR VERY LARGE 'MICROWAVE SAFE'
BOWL. COOK ON HIGH 3 TO 4 MINUTES. STIR WELL.
COOK 4 MORE MINUTES. STIR IN BUTTER AND VANILLA.
COOK ONE MINUTE MORE. ADD BAKING SODA AND GENTLY
STIR UNTIL LIGHT AND FOAMY. SPREAD MIXTURE
QUICKLY ON LIGHTLY GREASED COOKIE SHEET. COOL FOR
½ HOUR. BREAK INTO PIECES.

MEN WHO THINK WOMEN ARE THE WEAKER
SEX HAVE NEVER GONE SHOPPING WITH ONE.

B.L.'s COOKIES

GUESS WHAT! — YOU'RE ABOUT TO MAKE DAD'S COOKIES!

1 CUP BUTTER OR MARGARINE	250 mL
1 CUP WHITE SUGAR	250 mL
½ CUP BROWN SUGAR	125 mL
1 EGG	
1½ CUPS ROLLED OATS	375 mL
1½ CUPS FLOUR	375 mL
1 CUP COCONUT	250 mL
1 TSP. BAKING SODA	5 mL
1 TSP. BAKING POWDER	5 mL
2 TBSPS. MOLASSES	30 mL
1 TSP. VANILLA	5 mL
1½ TSPS. CINNAMON	7 mL
1 TSP. ALLSPICE	5 mL
1 TSP. NUTMEG	5 mL

COMBINE BUTTER AND SUGARS. ADD EGG THEN REMAINING INGREDIENTS. MIX WELL. ROLL IN SMALL BALLS AND PLACE ON COOKIE SHEET. DO NOT PRESS DOWN. BAKE AT 350° FOR 10 TO 12 MINUTES. MAKES 4 DOZEN.

SKINNY COOKS CAN'T BE TRUSTED.

ZUCCHINI COOKIES

THE GARDEN TURNED TO CALORIES!

¾ CUP MARGARINE	175 mL
1½ CUPS SUGAR	375 mL
1 EGG - BEATEN	
1 TSP. VANILLA	5 mL
1½ CUPS ZUCCHINI - GRATED	375 mL
2½ CUPS FLOUR	625 mL
2 TSPS. BAKING POWDER	10 mL
½ TSP. SALT	2 mL
1 TSP. CINNAMON	5 mL
1 CUP ALMONDS OR OTHER NUTS - CHOPPED	250 mL
1 CUP CHOCOLATE CHIPS	250 mL

CREAM MARGARINE AND SUGAR. ADD EGG, VANILLA THEN ZUCCHINI. ADD DRY INGREDIENTS, SPICES AND NUTS AND STIR IN CHOCOLATE CHIPS. DROP BY THE TEASPOONFUL ON A GREASED COOKIE SHEET. BAKE AT 350° FOR 12 TO 15 MINUTES.

BROKEN COOKIES DON'T HAVE CALORIES!

PEANUT BUTTER COOKIES

YOU ASKED FOR IT!

⅓	CUP SHORTENING OR MARGARINE	75 mL
½	CUP BROWN SUGAR	125 mL
½	CUP WHITE SUGAR	125 mL
½	CUP PEANUT BUTTER	125 mL
1	EGG - SLIGHTLY BEATEN	
1	CUP FLOUR	250 mL
1	TSP. BAKING SODA	5 mL
½	TSP. SALT	2 mL
	SUGAR FOR COATING	

CREAM SHORTENING AND SUGARS. ADD PEANUT BUTTER AND MIX WELL. ADD EGG AND THEN THE DRY INGREDIENTS. ROLL INTO BALLS AND ROLL IN SUGAR. PLACE ON GREASED COOKIE SHEET. PRESS FLAT WITH FORK. BAKE AT 350° FOR ABOUT 10 MINUTES. MAKES 3 DOZEN!

IT'S A SMALL WORLD - BUT I WOULDN'T WANT TO PAINT IT!

PECAN CRISPS

DELIGHTFUL!!

1	CUP BUTTER OR MARGARINE	250 mL
2	TSPS. VANILLA	10 mL
1	CUP ICING SUGAR	250 mL
1	CUP FLOUR	250 mL
1-	3 OZ. PKG. PECANS - CHOPPED	85 g

COMBINE BUTTER, VANILLA AND ICING SUGAR AND BEAT UNTIL SMOOTH AND LIGHT. BEAT IN FLOUR AND ADD NUTS. SPREAD BATTER ON A 15"x 11" BAKING SHEET. BAKE AT 350° FOR 18 MINUTES. SPRINKLE EVENLY WITH ICING SUGAR. CUT INTO SMALL PIECES WHILE WARM.

THE VELOCITY OF THE WIND IS DIRECTLY PROPORTIONAL TO THE PRICE OF THE HAIRDO!

POPPY SEED COOKIES

LIGHT, FLUFFY AND VERY DELICATE.

1	CUP BUTTER OR MARGARINE	250 mL
½	CUP SUGAR	125 mL
2	EGG YOLKS	
2	CUPS FLOUR	500 mL
¼	TSP. SALT	1 mL
3	TBSPS. POPPY SEEDS	45 mL
1	TSP. VANILLA	5 mL
	SUGAR	

PREHEAT OVEN TO 375°. GREASE A BAKING SHEET. CREAM BUTTER, SUGAR AND EGG YOLKS. ADD FLOUR SALT, POPPY SEEDS AND VANILLA. MIX WELL. CHILL DOUGH ONE HOUR. FORM DOUGH INTO TEASPOON SIZED BALLS. PLACE ON COOKIE SHEET AND DIP THE BOTTOM OF A JUICE GLASS INTO SUGAR AND PRESS BALLS FLAT. BAKE 8 TO 10 MINUTES. MAKES 4 DOZEN COOKIES.

ALWAYS YIELD TO TEMPTATION...
IT MIGHT NOT PASS YOUR WAY AGAIN.

FATAL ATTRACTIONS

A CAKE-LIKE COOKIE THAT'S IRRESISTIBLE!

4	SQUARES UNSWEETENED CHOCOLATE	120 g
½	CUP SHORTENING	125 mL
2	CUPS SUGAR	500 mL
2	TSPS. VANILLA	10 mL
4	EGGS	
2	CUPS FLOUR	500 mL
2	TSPS. BAKING POWDER	10 mL
1	CUP CHOCOLATE CHIPS	250 mL
½	CUP ICING SUGAR	125 mL

MELT CHOCOLATE SQUARES AND SHORTENING, BUT DO NOT BOIL. STIR IN SUGAR AND ALLOW TO COOL. SPOON MIXTURE INTO A BOWL, ADD VANILLA AND BEAT WELL. ADD EGGS, ONE AT A TIME, BEATING WELL AFTER EACH ADDITION. COMBINE FLOUR AND BAKING POWDER; ADD TO CREAMED MIXTURE. BEAT WELL. FOLD IN CHOCOLATE CHIPS. REFRIGERATE 1 HOUR. ROLL DOUGH INTO 1" BALLS AND ROLL IN ICING SUGAR UNTIL COATED. BAKE ON GREASED SHEETS AT 350°. 10 TO 12 MINUTES. MAKES ABOUT 5 DOZEN COOKIES.

NEVER OWN ANYTHING THAT EATS WHILE YOU SLEEP.

GINGER SNAPS

MAKES PERFECT GINGERBREAD MEN.

3/4 CUP MARGARINE OR SHORTENING	175 mL
1 CUP SUGAR	250 mL
1/4 CUP MOLASSES	50 mL
1 EGG – BEATEN	
2 CUPS FLOUR	500 mL
1/4 TSP. SALT	1 mL
2 TSPS. BAKING SODA	10 mL
1 TSP. CINNAMON	5 mL
1 TSP. CLOVES	5 mL
1 TSP. GINGER	5 mL
SUGAR	

CREAM TOGETHER MARGARINE AND SUGAR. ADD
MOLASSES AND EGG - BEAT TOGETHER. COMBINE
FLOUR, SALT, BAKING SODA AND SPICES. ADD TO CREAMED
MIXTURE. MIX WELL. ROLL INTO BALLS, THEN IN SUGAR.
PRESS FLAT WITH FORK. BAKE AT 375° FOR 15 MINUTES.
MAKES 4 DOZEN. (DEPENDING ON THE SIZE OF YOUR BALLS)

THE FIRST SIGN OF MATURITY IS THE
DISCOVERY THAT THE VOLUME KNOB ALSO TURNS LEFT.

MATRIMONIAL BARS

AT LAST— THE VERY THING FOR ALL THAT RHUBARB
YOU FROZE LAST FALL. OR— USE THE TRADITIONAL DATE
FILLING.

RHUBARB FILLING:

3 CUPS RHUBARB- CUT INTO ½" PIECES	750 mL
1½ CUPS SUGAR	375 mL
2 TBSPS. CORNSTARCH	30 mL
1 TSP. VANILLA	5 mL

OR DATE FILLING:

½ LB. CHOPPED DATES	250 g
½ CUP WATER	125 mL
2 TBSPS. BROWN SUGAR	30 mL
1 TSP. GRATED ORANGE RIND	5 mL
2 TBSPS. ORANGE JUICE	30 mL
1 TSP. LEMON JUICE	5 mL

THE CRUST:

1½ CUPS ROLLED OATS	375 mL
1½ CUPS FLOUR	375 mL
½ TSP. BAKING SODA	2 mL
1 TSP. BAKING POWDER	5 mL
¼ TSP. SALT	1 mL
1 CUP BROWN SUGAR	250 mL
1 CUP BUTTER	250 mL

FOR THE METHOD, REFER TO NEXT PAGE.

MATRIMONIAL BARS

THIS RECIPE CONTINUED FROM PAGE 170.

THE METHOD:

PRE-HEAT OVEN TO 350°. COMBINE FILLING INGREDIENTS AND COOK UNTIL THICK. IF MAKING DATE FILLING, ADD FRUIT JUICES AFTER COOKING. COOL COMPLETELY. COMBINE CRUST INGREDIENTS AND PAT 2/3 OF MIXTURE INTO A GREASED 9" x 9" PAN. ADD FILLING AND SPRINKLE WITH REMAINING CRUMBS. BAKE FOR 30 TO 35 MINUTES. CHILL BEFORE CUTTING.

CHOCOLATE PEANUT BUTTER BALLS

A CHRISTMAS FAVOURITE !

1	CUP PEANUT BUTTER	250 mL
1	CUP ICING SUGAR	250 mL
½	CUP NUTS - CHOPPED	125 mL
½	CUP RICE CRISPIES	125 mL
4	oz. SEMI-SWEET CHOCOLATE	120 g
1	TBSP. BUTTER	15 mL

MIX TOGETHER ALL INGREDIENTS AND CHILL IN FRIDGE FOR 10 TO 15 MINUTES. ROLL INTO BALLS. MELT CHOCOLATE WITH BUTTER. DIP BALLS IN CHOCOLATE AND CHILL.

BUTTER TART SLICE

A SLICE OF LIFE — ALL TARTS SHOULD TASTE AS GOOD!

THE CRUST:

2 CUPS FLOUR	500 mL
1/4 CUP WHITE SUGAR	50 mL
1 CUP BUTTER OR MARGARINE	250 mL
PINCH SALT	

THE FILLING:

3 EGGS — BEATEN	
2 CUPS BROWN SUGAR	500 mL
1/4 CUP BUTTER	50 mL
1 TBSP. BAKING POWDER	15 mL
PINCH SALT	
3/4 CUP COCONUT	175 mL
1 TSP. VANILLA	5 mL
1 CUP RAISINS	250 mL
3 TSPS. FLOUR	15 mL
NUTS — ARE OPTIONAL	

TO MAKE CRUST, COMBINE FIRST FOUR INGREDIENTS AND PRESS INTO 9" x 13" PAN.

TO MAKE FILLING, MELT BUTTER, ADD EGGS AND REMAINING INGREDIENTS. POUR OVER CRUST. BAKE AT 350° FOR 35 MINUTES. CUT WHILE HOT.

ROCKY MOUNTAIN SQUARE

ITS WICKED!

1- 16 OZ. PKG. CHOCOLATE CHIPS	500 mL
1 CUP BUTTER	250 mL
2 CUPS ICING SUGAR	500 mL
2 EGGS - BEATEN	
4 CUPS MINIATURE MARSHMALLOWS	1 L
GRAHAM WAFERS	

MIX FIRST FOUR INGREDIENTS TOGETHER AND MELT AT LOW HEAT. LET COOL SLIGHTLY AND ADD MARSHMALLOWS. LINE A 9"x 13" PAN WITH GRAHAM WAFERS. SPREAD MIXTURE OVER WAFERS AND SPRINKLE WITH ICING SUGAR. REFRIGERATE.

BUDGET: A MATHEMATICAL CONFIRMATION
OF YOUR SUSPICIONS.

PEANUT BUTTER BROWNIES

½ CUP BUTTER OR MARGARINE	125 mL
½ CUP SUGAR	125 mL
½ CUP DARK BROWN SUGAR – PACKED	125 mL
1 EGG – BEATEN	
⅓ CUP PEANUT BUTTER	75 mL
½ TSP. VANILLA	2 mL
1 CUP OATMEAL	250 mL
1 CUP FLOUR	250 mL
½ TSP. BAKING SODA	2 mL
¼ TSP. SALT	1 mL

ICING:

1 CUP ICING SUGAR	250 mL
½ CUP PEANUT BUTTER	125 mL
4 TO 6 TBSPS. MILK	60-90 mL

CREAM BUTTER AND SUGARS, ADD EGG, PEANUT BUTTER AND VANILLA. MIX WELL. STIR IN OATMEAL, FLOUR, BAKING SODA AND SALT. BAKE AT 350° FOR 25 TO 30 MINUTES IN A GREASED 9" x 9" PAN. COMBINE INGREDIENTS FOR ICING; BLEND WELL. ICE BROWNIES WHILE WARM. COOL AND ENJOY!

IT COSTS NO MORE TO GO FIRST CLASS —
YOU JUST CAN'T STAY AS LONG.

PICTURED ON OVERLEAF:

CHOCOLATE SABAYON - PAGE 189

STELLA BY STARLIGHT - PAGE 193

FUDGE PIE WITH CUSTARD SAUCE - PAGE 198

PECAN CUPS

SHELLS:

1 CUP MARGARINE OR BUTTER	250 mL
1 - 8 OZ. PKG. CREAM CHEESE	250 g
DASH SALT	
2 CUPS FLOUR	500 mL

FILLING:

2 EGGS	
1½ CUPS BROWN SUGAR - PACKED	375 mL
2 TBSPS. BUTTER - MELTED	30 mL
1½ CUPS PECANS - CHOPPED	375 mL
½ TSP. VANILLA	2 mL

TO MAKE SHELLS, BEAT BUTTER, CREAM CHEESE AND SALT UNTIL FLUFFY. ADD FLOUR AND CONTINUE TO MIX. PUT DOUGH IN REFRIGERATOR UNTIL FIRM TO HANDLE. AFTER CHILLING, FORM DOUGH INTO LITTLE BALLS AND PRESS INTO BOTTOM AND SIDES OF SMALL, LIGHTLY GREASED TART TINS.

TO MAKE FILLING, BEAT EGGS AND ADD ALL REMAINING INGREDIENTS AND SPOON INTO SHELLS. BAKE AT 350° FOR 30 MINUTES. MAKES 48 - 2" DIAMETER TARTS.

ENGLISH COOKING - IF IT'S WARM, IT'S BEER, IF IT'S COLD, IT'S FOOD!

SHORTBREAD TARTS
— WITH CHEESE 'N' FRUIT —

SO PRETTY TO LOOK AT — MORE FUN TO EAT!
SEE PICTURE, PAGE 157.

SHORTBREAD TARTS —

USE TINY MUFFIN TINS — APPROXIMATELY 1½" DIAMETER.
THIS WOULD YIELD ABOUT 3 DOZEN.

1 CUP BUTTER		250 mL
½ CUP ICING SUGAR		125 mL
1½ CUPS FLOUR		375 mL
1 TBSP. CORNSTARCH		15 mL

MIX INGREDIENTS IN MIXMASTER. DON'T ROLL BUT
PAT INTO MUFFIN TINS WITH YOUR FINGERS TO FORM
SHELLS. PRICK THE BOTTOMS WITH A FORK AND BAKE
20 MINUTES AT 300° TO 325°. DURING BAKING TIME, PRICK
BOTTOMS AGAIN IF THE SHELLS PUFF UP. THESE MAY BE
MADE IN LARGE QUANTITY AND FROZEN.

CHEESE 'N' FRUIT FILLING —

1 - 8 OZ. PKG. CREAM CHEESE — SOFTENED	250 g
1 CAN SWEETENED CONDENSED MILK (EAGLE BRAND)	300 mL
⅓ CUP LEMON JUICE	75 mL
1 TSP. VANILLA	5 mL

IN A LARGE BOWL BEAT CHEESE UNTIL FLUFFY.
GRADUALLY BEAT IN MILK. STIR IN LEMON JUICE AND
VANILLA.

O.K. NOW, FILL TARTS AT LEAST 2 HOURS BEFORE
SERVING TO ALLOW FLAVOURS TO BLEND. TOP WITH FRESH
FRUIT (I.E. KIWI, STRAWBERRIES).

PUMPKIN CHEESECAKE

A GRAND FINALE FOR THANKSGIVING DINNER.

CRUST:

1 CUP CRUSHED GINGERSNAPS	250 mL
3 TBSPS. BUTTER - MELTED	45 mL
1 TSP. CINNAMON	5 mL
2 TBSPS. BROWN SUGAR	30 mL

FILLING:

4 - 8 OZ. PKGS. CREAM CHEESE - SOFTENED	4 - 250 g
1½ CUPS SUGAR	375 mL
5 EGGS	
¼ CUP FLOUR	50 mL
2 TSPS. PUMPKIN PIE SPICE OR EQUAL PARTS GINGER, CINNAMON AND NUTMEG	10 mL
1 - 14 OZ. CAN PUMPKIN	398 mL
2 TBSPS. LIGHT RUM	30 mL
1 CUP WHIPPING CREAM - WHIPPED	250 mL

COMBINE CRUST INGREDIENTS. LIGHTLY GREASE A 10" SPRINGFORM PAN AND LINE BOTTOM WITH CRUMB MIXTURE. PAT FIRM AND CHILL. PREHEAT OVEN TO 325°. BEAT SOFTENED CREAM CHEESE TILL FLUFFY. SLOWLY BEAT IN SUGAR. ADD EGGS, ONE AT A TIME, BEATING WELL AFTER EACH ADDITION. GRADUALLY BEAT IN FLOUR, SPICES, PUMPKIN AND RUM. POUR BATTER OVER CRUST. BAKE FOR 1½ TO 1¾ HOURS OR TILL FILLING IS SET. COOL FOR AN HOUR. REFRIGERATE SEVERAL HOURS. GARNISH WITH WHIPPED CREAM AND A SPRINKLE OF CINNAMON. SERVES 10 TO 12.

FROSTY PEACH DESSERT

COOL, CREAMY AND SMOOTH.

1 CUP FLOUR	250 mL
1/3 CUP BROWN SUGAR	75 mL
1/4 TSP. CINNAMON	1 mL
1/2 CUP BUTTER – MELTED	125 mL
10 PEACHES	
1 CUP SUGAR	250 mL
2 EGG WHITES	
2 TBSPS. LEMON JUICE	30 mL
1 CUP WHIPPING CREAM – WHIPPED	250 mL

IN SHALLOW PAN, COMBINE FLOUR, BROWN SUGAR, CINNAMON AND MELTED BUTTER, MIXING WELL. BAKE IN 350° OVEN FOR 20 MINUTES, STIRRING 2 TO 3 TIMES TO KEEP MIXTURE CRUMBLY. LET COOL. RESERVE 1 CUP FOR TOPPING. SPREAD REMAINDER IN 9" SPRING-FORM PAN OR IN 9" x 13" BAKING PAN. PEEL AND STONE 4 PEACHES (THICK). SLICE THINLY AND PLACE IN LARGE, DEEP BOWL AND MASH WELL. ADD SUGAR, EGG WHITES, AND LEMON JUICE. BEAT AT MEDIUM SPEED UNTIL FOAMY, THEN AT HIGH SPEED UNTIL DOUBLED IN VOLUME AND MIXTURE HAS THICKENED – ABOUT 10 MINUTES. FOLD WHIPPED CREAM INTO PEACH MIXTURE. SPREAD OVER CRUMB MIXTURE. SPRINKLE RESERVED CRUMBS ON TOP. COVER AND FREEZE FOR AT LEAST 6 HOURS. TRANSFER TO FRIDGE 30 MINUTES BEFORE SERVING. TO SERVE, PEEL AND SLICE REMAINING PEACHES AND ARRANGE OVER EACH SERVING. SERVES 10.

RHUBARB DELIGHT

WHEN FRIENDS GIVE YOU "THE RHUBARB"

CRUST:

1	CUP FLOUR	250 mL
1/4	TSP. SALT	1 mL
2	TBSPS. SUGAR	30 mL
1/2	CUP BUTTER	125 mL

MIX TOGETHER AND PUT INTO A 8" x 8" CAKE PAN. BAKE AT 325° FOR 10 MINUTES OR UNTIL LIGHTLY BROWNED.

FILLING:

1	CUP SUGAR	250 mL
2	TBSPS. FLOUR	30 mL
1/3	CUP CREAM	75 mL
3	EGG YOLKS	
2 1/4	CUPS RED RHUBARB - CUT VERY FINE	560 mL

MIX ALL INGREDIENTS AND COOK OVER LOW HEAT UNTIL THICK. POUR INTO CRUST.

MERINGUE:

3	EGG WHITES	
1/4	TSP. CREAM OF TARTAR	1 mL
6	TBSPS. SUGAR	90 mL

BEAT EGG WHITES AND CREAM OF TARTAR UNTIL FOAMY. GRADUALLY ADD THE SUGAR, ABOUT 2 TBSPS. AT A TIME, BEATING BETWEEN ADDITIONS. CONTINUE BEATING UNTIL MERINGUE IS THICK AND GLOSSY AND SUGAR IS ALL DISSOLVED. MERINGUE SHOULD BE SMOOTH AND STAND IN STIFF PEAKS. SPREAD MERINGUE OVER THE FILLING. BAKE AT 400° UNTIL LIGHTLY BROWNED.

RHUBARB CRISP WITH BOURBON SAUCE

FOR THOSE OF US NORTH OF THE BORDER, RUM OR BRANDY CAN BE SUBSTITUTED.

RHUBARB CRISP—

¾ CUP BROWN SUGAR-FIRMLY PACKED	175 mL
¾ CUP FLOUR	175 mL
⅓ CUP BUTTER-SOFTENED	75 mL
1 TSP. CINNAMON	5 mL
6 CUPS FRESH OR FROZEN RHUBARB-DICED	1.5 kg
⅓ TO ⅔ CUP WHITE SUGAR	75-150 mL
GRATED RIND OF 1 LEMON	

BOURBON SAUCE—

3 EGG YOLKS	
⅓ CUP WHITE SUGAR	75 mL
1 CUP WHIPPING CREAM	250 mL
⅓ CUP MILK	75 mL
¼ CUP BOURBON	50 mL
PINCH SALT	

TO MAKE THE CRISP—COMBINE FIRST 4 INGREDIENTS UNTIL CRUMBLY. IN A 2 QT. CASSEROLE COMBINE RHUBARB, SUGAR AND LEMON RIND. COVER WITH FIRST MIXTURE. BAKE 1 HOUR AT 350°. SERVES 8.

TO MAKE SAUCE— IN TOP OF DOUBLE BOILER, BEAT YOLKS AND SUGAR UNTIL LIGHT AND LEMON COLOURED. WHISK IN CREAM AND MILK. COOK OVER HOT WATER (NOT BOILING) UNTIL MIXTURE COATS A SPOON. STIR IN BOURBON AND SALT. COOK 5 MINUTES. SERVE WARM. MAKES 2 CUPS.

TOFFEE MERINGUE

MAKE MERINGUES IN ADVANCE AND YOU WILL HAVE AN EASY DESSERT.

2 PKGS. MᴬᶜINTOSH TOFFEE	56 g EACH
4 EGG WHITES	
1 CUP SUGAR	250 mL
½ TSP. VANILLA	2 mL
1 TSP. VINEGAR	5 mL
2 CUPS WHIPPING CREAM-SWEETEN TO TASTE	500 mL
CHOCOLATE CURLS	

PREHEAT OVEN TO 275°. PUT TOFFEE IN FREEZER TILL FROZEN. CUT OUT 2-9" BROWN PAPER CIRCLES AND PLACE ON A COOKIE SHEET. WHIP EGG WHITES UNTIL THEY FORM PEAKS. GRADUALLY ADD SUGAR, VANILLA, VINEGAR AND CONTINUE BEATING UNTIL STIFF. SPREAD EGG MIXTURE IN 2-8" CIRCLES. (MIXTURE WILL EXPAND DURING BAKING.) BAKE 1 HOUR. TURN OVEN OFF AND LEAVE MERINGUES TO DRY FOR SEVERAL HOURS. DO NOT OPEN OVEN. WHEN READY TO SERVE, CRUSH TOFFEE - A HAMMER WORKS WELL! ADD TO WHIPPED CREAM. SPREAD ½ OF MIXTURE BETWEEN 1ˢᵀ AND 2ᴺᴰ MERINGUE. TOP WITH REMAINING CREAM. GARNISH WITH CHOCOLATE CURLS.

CHOCOLATE MOUSSE CAKE

TOTALLY DECADENT!

THE CAKE:

7- 1oz. SQUARES SEMI-SWEET CHOCOLATE	7-30 g
1/4 LB. BUTTER	115 g
7 EGGS - SEPARATED	
1 CUP SUGAR	250 mL
1 TSP. VANILLA	5 mL

THE BEST PART:

1 oz. KAHLUA	30 mL
1 oz. TIA MARIA	30 mL

THE FROSTING:

1 CUP WHIPPING CREAM	250 mL
1/3 CUP ICING SUGAR	75 mL
1 TSP. KAHLUA	5 mL

PREHEAT OVEN TO 325°. MELT CHOCOLATE AND
BUTTER OVER LOW HEAT. IN A BOWL, BEAT EGG YOLKS
AND 3/4 CUP OF SUGAR UNTIL VERY LIGHT AND FLUFFY,
AT LEAST 5 MINUTES. SLOWLY BEAT IN WARM CHOCOLATE
MIXTURE AND VANILLA. IN ANOTHER LARGE BOWL BEAT
EGG WHITES UNTIL SOFT PEAKS FORM. ADD 1/4 CUP OF
SUGAR, 1 TBSP. AT A TIME, BEATING CONSTANTLY FOR
10 MINUTES. CAREFULLY FOLD CHOCOLATE MIXTURE INTO
THE EGG WHITES.

YOU'LL WANT TO FINISH THIS - SEE NEXT PAGE.

CHOCOLATE MOUSSE CAKE

THIS RECIPE CONTINUED FROM PAGE 184.

RESERVE 1½ CUPS OF BATTER, COVER AND REFRIGERATE. POUR THE REST OF THE BATTER INTO A 9" SPRINGFORM PAN. BAKE CAKE FOR 35 MINUTES AND COOL. CAKE WILL DROP AND PULL AWAY FROM THE SIDES OF THE PAN. REMOVE OUTSIDE RING OF PAN. SPRINKLE LIQUEURS OVER CAKE, THEN SPREAD RESERVED BATTER ON TOP OF CAKE. REFRIGERATE UNTIL FIRM. PREPARE FROSTING BY BEATING WHIPPING CREAM UNTIL SOFT PEAKS FORM. ADD ICING SUGAR AND KAHLUA. SPREAD FROSTING OVER TOP AND SIDES OF CAKE. FREEZE UNCOVERED TILL FROZEN, THEN WRAP WITH FOIL. REMOVE FROM FREEZER 15 MINUTES BEFORE SERVING 8 TO 10.

ONE OF LIFE'S GREATEST DISAPPOINTMENTS IS FINDING THAT THE GUY WHO WRITES THE ADS FOR THE BANK IS NOT THE SAME GUY WHO MAKES THE LOANS.

TIRAMISU

THIS MEANS "IT LIFTS ME UP" A FAVOURITE
FROM LA CHAUMIERE RESTAURANT, IN CALGARY.

4 EGGS – SEPARATED	
¾ CUP SUGAR	175 mL
2-8 oz. CREAM CHEESE – SOFTENED	500 g
½ CUP COFFEE (½ CUP WATER WITH	
1 TSP. INSTANT COFFEE)	125 mL
¼ CUP KAHLUA OR RUM	50 mL
1 PKG. LADY FINGER COOKIES OR	
VANILLA WAFERS	250 g
2 – 1 oz. SQUARES SEMI-SWEET CHOCOLATE –	
FINELY GRATED	55 g

BEAT YOLKS IN MEDIUM SIZE BOWL, ADDING
SUGAR GRADUALLY UNTIL WELL MIXED, (NO GRITTY
FEELING IS LEFT.) ADD CREAM CHEESE AND MIX
WELL. BEAT EGG WHITES IN DEEP BOWL UNTIL
SOFT PEAKS FORM. FOLD INTO CHEESE MIXTURE.
SPREAD ¼ OF CHEESE MIXTURE INTO 12 CUP LARGE
BOWL. DIP LADY FINGERS IN MIXTURE OF KAHLUA &
COFFEE AND COVER CHEESE LAYER. REPEAT 3
TIMES USING CHOCOLATE ON EACH AND ENDING WITH
CHEESE AND CHOCOLATE. REFRIGERATE 6 HOURS OR
OVERNIGHT. SERVE CHILLED TO 8 TO 10 UPLIFTED
GUESTS.

1	CUP VANILLA WAFER COOKIE CRUMBS (24 WAFERS)	250 mL
½	CUP TOASTED ALMONDS - FINELY CHOPPED	125 mL
¼	CUP BUTTER - MELTED	50 mL
4	CUPS FRESH STRAWBERRIES	1 L
12	OZ. GOOD QUALITY WHITE CHOCOLATE	375 g
4	OZ. CREAM CHEESE	125 g
¼	CUP SUGAR	50 mL
¼	CUP ORANGE LIQUEUR OR FROZEN ORANGE JUICE CONCENTRATE	50 mL
1	TSP. VANILLA	5 mL
2	CUPS WHIPPING CREAM	500 mL
2	TBSPS. COCOA POWDER	25 mL

COMBINE WAFER CRUMBS, ALMONDS AND BUTTER. PRESS INTO BOTTOM OF 9" SPRINGFORM PAN. WASH, DRY AND HULL BERRIES. RESERVE A FEW FOR GARNISH. CHOP CHOCOLATE AND MELT IN DOUBLE BOILER OR MICRO-WAVE. SPREAD 3 TBSPS. CHOCOLATE OVER COOKIE BASE. ARRANGE WHOLE BERRIES, POINTS UP, ON BASE. REFRIGERATE. ALLOW REMAINING CHOCOLATE TO COOL SLIGHTLY. BEAT CHEESE UNTIL SMOOTH, THEN BEAT IN SUGAR. MIX IN LIQUEUR (OR JUICE) AND VANILLA. SLOWLY BEAT IN REMAINING CHOCOLATE. WHIP CREAM. STIR ABOUT ⅓ INTO CHOCOLATE MIXTURE AND FOLD IN THE REMAINDER. POUR OVER BERRIES, SHAKING PAN GENTLY TO FILL IN BETWEEN BERRIES. REFRIGERATE 3 HOURS OR OVERNIGHT. TO REMOVE, RUN KNIFE CAREFULLY AROUND EDGE AND GENTLY REMOVE FROM SPRINGFORM. DUST WITH COCOA AND GARNISH WITH RESERVED STRAWBERRIES.

CRÈME CARAMEL

A GOURMET TOUCH THAT CAN BE MADE THE DAY BEFORE.

CARAMEL —

¾	CUP WATER	175 mL
1	CUP SUGAR	250 mL

PLACE WATER AND SUGAR IN SAUCEPAN; STIR OVER LOW HEAT UNTIL SUGAR DISSOLVES; INCREASE HEAT AND BRING TO BOIL. BOIL APPROXIMATELY 10 TO 15 MINUTES UNTIL MIXTURE TURNS GOLDEN BROWN AND CARAMELIZES. WATCH CLOSELY AS IT WILL BURN VERY EASILY. POUR CARAMEL INTO 8 INDIVIDUAL SOUFFLÉ DISHES. (RAMEKINS.) ROTATE DISHES QUICKLY SO CARAMEL EVENLY COATS SIDES AND BASE OF DISH.

CUSTARD —

4	WHOLE EGGS	
3	EGG YOLKS	
1	TSP. VANILLA	5 mL
½	CUP SUGAR	125 mL
3	CUPS CREAM	750 mL

IN LARGE BOWL BEAT TOGETHER WHOLE EGGS, EGG YOLKS, VANILLA AND SUGAR UNTIL LEMON COLOURED. SCALD CREAM IN SAUCEPAN AND ALLOW TO COOL SLIGHTLY. POUR CREAM INTO EGG MIXTURE, STIRRING CONSTANTLY. POUR CUSTARD MIXTURE EVENLY INTO EACH DISH. SET DISHES IN SHALLOW BAKING PAN CONTAINING 1" WATER. BAKE CUSTARDS AT 325° FOR 35 TO 40 MINUTES UNTIL CUSTARD IS SET. COOL IN REFRIGERATOR FOR SEVERAL HOURS. JUST BEFORE SERVING, SET DISHES IN HOT WATER AND EASE CUSTARDS AWAY FROM SIDES OF DISH. INVERT ONTO SERVING PLATES.

CHOCOLATE SABAYON

4	EGG YOLKS	
1/2	CUP SUGAR	125 mL
1/2	CUP WINE - WHITE	125 mL
1/4	CUP UNSWEETENED COCOA - SIFTED	50 mL
1	CUP WHIPPING CREAM	250 mL
2	TBSPS. COFFEE LIQUEUR	30 mL

IN A DOUBLE BOILER (NOT ALUMINUM), BEAT EGG YOLKS AND SUGAR WITH ELECTRIC BEATER OVER MEDIUM HEAT FOR 2 MINUTES OR UNTIL SLIGHTLY THICKENED. IN A SMALL BOWL, WHISK WINE AND COCOA. ADD TO EGG MIXTURE AND BEAT FOR 2 TO 3 MINUTES ON HIGH UNTIL MIXTURE HAS TRIPLED IN VOLUME AND COATS BACK OF SPOON. REMOVE FROM HEAT AND PLACE IN LARGE BOWL - LET COOL. WHIP OCCASIONALLY. WHIP CREAM AND FOLD IN LIQUEUR. GENTLY FOLD INTO CHOCOLATE MIXTURE. SPOON INTO YOUR PRETTIEST SHERBET DISHES. SEE PICTURE, PAGE 175.

TELLING YOUR TEENAGER THE FACTS OF LIFE IS LIKE GIVING A FISH A BATH!

LEMON SORBET

THIS IS A DELIGHTFUL FINALE TO A SUMPTUOUS MEAL. IF YOU REALLY WANT TO SHOW OFF - SERVE BETWEEN COURSES TO 'CLEANSE' THE PALATE - LAH DE DAH!

1 CUP MILK (2% OR SKIM WILL DO)	250 mL
1 CUP WHIPPING CREAM	250 mL
5 LEMONS = 1 CUP LEMON JUICE	250 mL
⅔ CUP BERRY SUGAR (FINE GRANULATED)	150 mL

CUT IN HALF AND SQUEEZE LEMONS; SAVE SHELLS. MIX ALL INGREDIENTS TOGETHER IN A SHALLOW DISH AND FREEZE FOR 4 HOURS. STIR OCCASIONALLY TO BREAK UP ICE CRYSTALS. SPOON INTO LEMON SHELLS, COVER AND RETURN TO FREEZER UNTIL READY TO SERVE. (HINT - CUT ENDS OFF RINDS SO THEY WON'T "ROCK AND ROLL" WHEN YOU SERVE THEM.) GARNISH WITH A MINT LEAF. SEE PICTURE, PAGE 157.

BE LIKE A DUCK - ABOVE THE SURFACE LOOK COMPOSED AND UNRUFFLED - BELOW THE SURFACE, PADDLE LIKE CRAZY.

DARK CHOCOLATE CAKE

PARDON THE PACKAGES – YOUR GUESTS CERTAINLY WILL!

1 – 18 oz. PKG. DARK DEVILS FOOD CAKE MIX	520 g
1 – 3¾ oz. PKG. INSTANT CHOCOLATE PUDDING MIX	113 g
1 CUP SOUR CREAM	250 mL
½ CUP COOKING OIL	125 mL
½ CUP WARM WATER	125 mL
4 EGGS – BEATEN	
1½ CUPS SEMI-SWEET CHOCOLATE CHIPS	375 mL

IN LARGE BOWL COMBINE ALL INGREDIENTS EXCEPT CHOCOLATE CHIPS. BEAT 4 MINUTES. FOLD IN CHIPS. BAKE IN GREASED AND FLOURED 12 CUP BUNDT PAN AT 350° FOR 50 TO 60 MINUTES OR UNTIL TOOTHPICK COMES OUT CLEAN. COOL IN PAN FOR 15 MINUTES THEN TURN OUT ONTO SERVING PLATE. DUST WITH ICING SUGAR – IF YOU WANT TO REALLY MAKE THINGS DIFFICULT!

POPPY SEED CHIFFON CAKE

½ CUP POPPY SEEDS	125 mL
1 CUP BOILING WATER	250 mL
2 CUPS FLOUR	500 mL
1½ CUPS SUGAR	375 mL
1 TBSP. BAKING POWDER	15 mL
1 TSP. SALT	5 mL
½ CUP SALAD OIL	125 mL
2 TSPS. VANILLA	10 mL
7 EGGS – SEPARATED	
¼ TSP. BAKING SODA	1 mL
½ TSP. CREAM OF TARTAR	2 mL

SOAK POPPY SEEDS IN BOILING WATER UNTIL LUKEWARM. IN A BOWL, SIFT TOGETHER FLOUR, SUGAR, BAKING POWDER AND SALT. FORM A WELL IN CENTRE AND ADD OIL, POPPY SEEDS WITH WATER, VANILLA, EGG YOLKS AND SODA. BEAT UNTIL SMOOTH. IN ANOTHER BOWL BEAT EGG WHITES WITH CREAM OF TARTAR UNTIL STIFF PEAKS FORM. POUR YOLK MIXTURE OVER EGG WHITES, AND GENTLY FOLD. (DO NOT STIR.) POUR INTO UNGREASED 10" TUBE PAN. BAKE AT 350° FOR 60 MINUTES. INVERT PAN TO COOL.

FOR THE ICING, SEE NEXT PAGE.

POPPY SEED CHIFFON CAKE

THIS RECIPE CONTINUED FROM PAGE 192.

ICING:

1	PT. WHIPPING CREAM	500 mL
½	CUP SUGAR	125 mL
2	TSPS. VANILLA	10 mL
2 to 3	TSPS. COCOA - SIFTED	10-15 mL

WHIP CREAM. ADD SUGAR, THEN ADD VANILLA AND COCOA. BLEND WELL. STORE IN FRIDGE AND ICE CAKE AS AS CLOSE TO SERVING TIME AS POSSIBLE!

STELLA BY STARLIGHT

A SIMPLE, DELICATE SABAYON. BEAUTIFUL WITHOUT BEING FLAMBOYANT.

6	EGG YOLKS	
⅓	CUP SUGAR	75 mL
8 OZ.	WHITE WINE (ANY KIND WILL DO)	250 mL
	LEMON ZEST FOR GARNISH	

STELLA JUST PUTS ALL THIS IN A HEAVY 4 QT. POT OVER MEDIUM-HIGH HEAT AND BEATS THE DAYLIGHTS OUT OF IT. (USE AN ELECTRIC BEATER.) THIS TAKES ABOUT 5 MINUTES. IT SHOULD BE LIGHT AND FLUFFY AND FILL THE POT. SERVE IMMEDIATELY, TOPPED WITH LEMON ZEST. MAY BE SPOONED OVER FRESH FRUIT. SERVES 8 TO 10. SEE THE PICTURE, PAGE 175.

HAZELNUT TORTE

HAZEL MIGHT BE A NUT — BUT SHE KNOWS HER TORTES.
A GOURMET BREEZE — AND BEST OF ALL, YOU CAN MAKE IT
AND FREEZE UP TO 2 WEEKS IN ADVANCE. PICTURE — 157.

CAKE —

1/4	CUP FLOUR	50 mL
1/2	TSP. BAKING POWDER	2 mL
1/4	TSP. CINNAMON	1 mL
1/2	CUP BUTTER	125 mL
2/3	CUP SUGAR	150 mL
3	EGGS — SEPARATED	
1	CUP TOASTED, FINELY GROUND HAZELNUTS (FILBERTS)	250 mL
3	TBSPS. HAZELNUT LIQUEUR (FRANGELICO OR GRAND MARNIER)	45 mL

FILLING —

1 1/2	CUPS WHIPPING CREAM	375 mL
1/4	CUP SUGAR	50 mL
2	TBSPS. HAZELNUTS (FILBERTS) — TOASTED, FINELY GROUND	30 mL

GREASE AN 8" ROUND CAKE PAN. LINE BOTTOM WITH
GREASED WAXED PAPER. IN A BOWL, STIR TOGETHER
FLOUR, BAKING POWDER AND CINNAMON. SET ASIDE.
IN A LARGE BOWL, BEAT BUTTER AND 2/3 CUP SUGAR
UNTIL FLUFFY. BEAT IN EGG YOLKS. ADD FLOUR
MIXTURE; BEAT WELL. STIR IN 1/2 CUP OF GROUND NUTS.
IN A BOWL (USING CLEAN BEATERS) BEAT EGG WHITES
TILL STIFF PEAKS FORM. FOLD INTO CAKE BATTER.
TURN BATTER INTO PAN (IT WON'T BE RUNNY).

THAT'S NOT ALL, SEE NEXT PAGE.

HAZELNUT TORTE

THIS RECIPE CONTINUED FROM PAGE 194.

BAKE AT 350° FOR 35 MINUTES OR UNTIL WOODEN TOOTHPICK (WHAT OTHER KIND IS THERE?) COMES OUT CLEAN. COOL ON WIRE RACK FOR 10 MINUTES. REMOVE CAKE FROM PAN; REMOVE WAXED PAPER. DON'T PANIC— IT'S A SHALLOW CAKE. DRIZZLE LIQUEUR OVER TOP. SET IN FRIDGE TO CHILL. WHEN THOROUGHLY CHILLED, SLICE HORIZONTALLY IN 2 LAYERS. TRANSFER ONE LAYER TO CAKE PLATE. WHIP CREAM WITH 1/4 CUP SUGAR. MIX REMAINING 1/2 CUP NUTS WITH HALF THE CREAM AND USE AS FILLING BETWEEN CAKE LAYERS. SPREAD RESERVED CREAM OVER TOP AND SIDES OF CAKE. SPRINKLE 2 TBSPS. OF NUTS ON TOP.

TO FREEZE: PLACE UNCOVERED CAKE IN FREEZER FOR 30 MINUTES TILL CREAM FROSTING IS FROZEN. WRAP CAKE IN 3 LAYERS OF PLASTIC WRAP AND FREEZE UNTIL READY TO USE. THAW WRAPPED CAKE IN FRIDGE OVER- NIGHT. SERVES 12.

MOCHA WHIPPED CREAM CAKE

EASY AND SHOWY.

CAKE:

5	EGGS - SEPARATED (SHOULD BE ROOM TEMPERATURE)	
1	CUP SUGAR	250 mL
1	TSP. VANILLA	5 mL
½	TSP. INSTANT COFFEE : DISSOLVED IN	2 mL
3	TBSPS. BOILING WATER	45 mL
1	CUP FLOUR	250 mL
1	TSP. BAKING POWDER	5 mL

FROSTING:

2	CUPS WHIPPING CREAM	500 mL
2	TBSPS. BROWN SUGAR	30 mL
¼	CUP STRONG, COLD COFFEE	50 mL
2	TBSPS. COFFEE LIQUEUR	30 mL
¼	CUP TOASTED ALMONDS FOR GARNISH	50 mL

PREHEAT OVEN TO 350°. COMBINE EGG YOLKS AND SUGAR IN LARGE BOWL AND BEAT UNTIL THICK AND LEMON COLOURED (5 MINUTES). BLEND IN VANILLA AND DISSOLVED INSTANT COFFEE. COMBINE FLOUR AND BAKING POWDER AND BLEND INTO BATTER. BEAT EGG WHITES UNTIL STIFF. FOLD INTO BATTER. TURN INTO UNGREASED 10" TUBE PAN. BAKE 30 MINUTES. INVERT ONTO RACK AND LET STAND UNTIL COMPLETELY COOL.

FOR FROSTING SEE NEXT PAGE.

Mocha Whipped Cream Cake

THIS RECIPE CONTINUED FROM PAGE 196.

For frosting, whip cream with sugar until soft peaks form. Add coffee and liqueur and beat until stiff. Cut cake into 3 layers. Use about ⅓ frosting to fill layers and remainder to frost entire cake. Sprinke with toasted almonds. Chill four hours before serving.

Peaches and Cream Pie

1 - 9" PIE SHELL - UNBAKED	
3 CUPS. PEACHES - PEELED & SLICED	750 mL
½ CUP SUGAR	125 mL
3 TBSPS. FLOUR	45 mL
¼ TSP. CINNAMON	1 mL
PINCH OF SALT	A LITTLE
1 CUP SOUR CREAM	250 mL
¼ CUP BROWN SUGAR	50 mL

Arrange peaches in pastry shell. Combine sugar, flour, cinnamon, salt and sour cream. Beat mixture until smooth and pour over peaches. Bake at 425° for 15 minutes. Reduce heat to 350° and bake 35 minutes longer, or until filling is set. Sprinkle brown sugar over top and place under broiler until melted. Cool slightly before serving.

FUDGE PIE WITH CUSTARD SAUCE

RICH AND DELICIOUS! SEE PICTURE, PAGE 175.

½	CUP BUTTER	125 mL
2 - 1oz.	SQUARES UNSWEETENED CHOCOLATE	55 g
2	EGGS	
1	CUP SUGAR	250 mL
¼	CUP FLOUR	50 mL
¼	TSP. SALT	1 mL
1	TSP. VANILLA	5 mL
¾	CUP PECANS - CHOPPED (OPTIONAL)	

MELT BUTTER AND CHOCOLATE OVER LOW HEAT. COMBINE REMAINING INGREDIENTS. ADD CHOCOLATE MIXTURE AND BEAT UNTIL SMOOTH. POUR INTO A WELL BUTTERED 8" PIE PLATE. BAKE AT 350° FOR 25 TO 30 MINUTES.

CUSTARD SAUCE:
GET OUT YOUR WHISK!

1	CUP MILK	250 mL
1	CUP WHIPPING CREAM	250 mL
¾	CUP SUGAR	175 mL
6	EGG YOLKS - SLIGHTLY BEATEN	
2	TBSPS. GRAND MARNIER OR	
	ANY ORANGE FLAVOURED LIQUEUR	30 mL

TAKE YOUR WHISK AND SEE NEXT PAGE.

FUDGE PIE WITH CUSTARD SAUCE

THIS RECIPE CONTINUED FROM PAGE 198.

IN A HEAVY SAUCEPAN OVER MEDIUM-HIGH HEAT, BRING MILK, CREAM AND SUGAR TO A FULL BOIL. WHISKING CONSTANTLY, ADD 1/4 OF THE HOT CREAM MIXTURE IN A SLOW, STEADY STREAM TO EGG YOLKS. REDUCE HEAT TO MEDIUM. WHISK WARM EGG YOLK MIXTURE SLOWLY INTO REMAINING CREAM MIXTURE. WHISKING CONSTANTLY, COOK UNTIL MIXTURE THICKENS AND COATS BACK OF METAL SPOON (ABOUT 3 MINUTES— THIS HAPPENS ALL OF A SUDDEN). DO NOT OVER COOK OR EGGS WILL SCRAMBLE. REMOVE SAUCE FROM HEAT; WHISK 3 MINUTES UNTIL SLIGHTLY COOL. WHISK IN LIQUEUR (THAT IS, IF YOUR WHISK ISN'T BROKEN YET), THEN STRAIN. PLACE PLASTIC WRAP OVER CUSTARD; REFRIGERATE UNTIL CHILLED. TO SERVE, PUT SAUCE ON PLATE FIRST, THEN A SLICE OF PIE ON TOP; — AT ANY RATE, THAT'S THE WAY WE WOULD DO IT!

NO FOOD TASTES AS GOOD AS THE FOOD YOU EAT WHEN YOU'RE CHEATING ON A DIET.

PALACE PIE

A ROYAL TREAT!

1 - 9" BAKED PIE CRUST	
1 EGG - SLIGHTLY BEATEN	
1 CUP ICING SUGAR	250 mL
1/4 CUP BUTTER OR MARGARINE - SOFTENED	50 mL
1/4 TSP. VANILLA EXTRACT	1 mL
1 1/2 CUPS WHIPPING CREAM	375 mL
1/2 CUP STRAWBERRIES - SLICED OR	125 mL
2/3 CUP CRUSHED PINEAPPLE - WELL DRAINED	150 mL
1/4 CUP CHOPPED MARASCHINO CHERRIES -	
WELL DRAINED	50 mL
1/4 CUP CHOPPED PECANS OR SLIVERED ALMONDS	50 mL
MARASCHINO CHERRY HALVES - WELL DRAINED	

IN A SMALL BOWL, COMBINE EGG, ICING SUGAR, BUTTER AND VANILLA. BEAT WITH AN ELECTRIC MIXER UNTIL LIGHT AND CREAMY. SPREAD EVENLY IN BAKED PIE CRUST. IN A MEDIUM BOWL, WHIP CREAM UNTIL SOFT PEAKS FORM. FOLD IN STRAWBERRIES OR PINEAPPLE, MARASCHINO CHERRIES AND NUTS. SPREAD EVENLY OVER ICING SUGAR MIXTURE. REFRIGERATE TWO HOURS. GARNISH WITH MARASCHINO CHERRY HALVES. MAKES ABOUT 8 SERVINGS.

FRENCH LEMON PIE

4	EGGS	
1	CUP LIGHT CORN SYRUP	250 mL
1	TSP. GRATED LEMON PEEL	5 mL
1/3	CUP LEMON JUICE	75 mL
2	TBSPS. MELTED BUTTER	30 mL
1/2	CUP SUGAR	125 mL
2	TBSPS. FLOUR	30 mL
1	UNBAKED 9" PIE SHELL	
1/2	CUP WHIPPING CREAM	125 mL

IN A MEDIUM BOWL, BEAT EGGS WELL; ADD CORN SYRUP, LEMON PEEL, LEMON JUICE AND MELTED BUTTER. COMBINE SUGAR AND FLOUR, THEN STIR INTO EGG MIXTURE. POUR INTO UNBAKED PASTRY SHELL AND BAKE AT 350°F. FOR 50 MINUTES. CHILL. TO SERVE, WHIP CREAM AND MOUND ONTO PIE.

A MAN CLAIMS HIS WIFE LOST HER CREDIT CARDS BUT HE HASN'T REPORTED IT BECAUSE WHOEVER STOLE THEM SPENDS LESS THAN SHE DID.

TIN ROOF PIE

TAKES ONLY MINUTES - AND THEY'LL ASK FOR SECONDS.

¼	CUP PEANUT BUTTER	50 mL
¼	CUP LIGHT CORN SYRUP	50 mL
2	CUPS CORNFLAKES - CRUSHED	500 mL
1	QT. VANILLA ICE CREAM - SOFTENED	1 L
3	TBSPS. UNSALTED PEANUTS - CHOPPED	45 mL
	CHOCOLATE SYRUP - HEATED	

IN A 9" PIE PLATE, COMBINE PEANUT BUTTER AND CORN SYRUP. ADD CEREAL AND MIX UNTIL WELL COMBINED. PRESS INTO BOTTOM AND SIDES OF PLATE. CHILL. SPOON SOFTENED ICE CREAM INTO SHELL. SPRINKLE WITH CHOPPED NUTS. FREEZE. REMOVE FROM FREEZER 1 HOUR BEFORE SERVING. SERVE WITH WARM CHOCOLATE SYRUP. SERVES 6 TO 8, IF YOU DON'T INVITE ELEPHANTS.

I DON'T CARE WHAT THE WORLD KNOWS ABOUT ME,
I JUST HOPE MY MOTHER NEVER FINDS OUT.

CHOCOLATE PECAN PIE

BEWARE! RICH AND APPEALING TO TRUE CHOCOLATE LOVERS.

1 - 9" PASTRY SHELL - UNBAKED	
3 EGGS - SLIGHTLY BEATEN	
1 CUP CORN SYRUP	250 mL
4 - 1 oz. SQUARES SEMI-SWEET CHOCOLATE - MELT & COOL	4 - 30 g
1/3 CUP SUGAR	75 mL
2 TBSPS. BUTTER - MELTED	30 mL
1 TSP. VANILLA	5 mL
1 1/2 CUPS PECAN HALVES	375 mL

IN A LARGE BOWL STIR EGGS, CORN SYRUP, CHOCOLATE, SUGAR, MELTED BUTTER AND VANILLA UNTIL WELL BLENDED. STIR IN PECANS. POUR INTO PASTRY SHELL. BAKE AT 350° FOR 50 TO 60 MINUTES OR UNTIL KNIFE COMES OUT CLEAN. TOP WITH WHIPPING CREAM, OR ICE CREAM. (GILDING THE LILY).

A LOT OF GOOD ARGUMENTS ARE SPOILED
BY SOME GUY WHO KNOWS WHAT HE'S TALKING ABOUT!

RHUBARB MERINGUE PIE

1	9" UNBAKED PIE SHELL	
4	CUPS RHUBARB - FINELY CHOPPED	1 L
3	EGGS - SEPARATED	
1	CUP SUGAR	250 mL
2	TBSPS. FLOUR	30 mL
2	TBSPS. MELTED BUTTER	30 mL
1/3	CUP SUGAR	75 mL

COMBINE RHUBARB AND EGG YOLKS. ADD SUGAR AND FLOUR AND MIX WELL. STIR IN BUTTER AND SPOON INTO PIE SHELL. BAKE AT 350° FOR 30 MINUTES OR UNTIL SET. TO MAKE MERINGUE, BEAT EGG WHITES UNTIL SOFT PEAKS FORM. CONTINUE BEATING AND SLOWLY ADD SUGAR UNTIL MIXTURE IS THICK AND GLOSSY. HEAP LIGHTLY OVER PIE AND SPREAD TO EDGES OF THE CRUST. BROWN IN A 350° OVEN FOR ABOUT 10 MINUTES.

I KNOW A SECRETARY WHO CAN TYPE 20 LETTERS AN HOUR. HER BOSS IS STILL WAITING FOR HER TO LEARN THE OTHER 6.

PECAN CRUST ICE CREAM PIE
WITH CARAMEL SAUCE

WELL WORTH THE EFFORT!

CRUST

1	EGG WHITE - SAVE YOLK FOR CARAMEL SAUCE	
¼	TSP. SALT	1 mL
¼	CUP SUGAR	50 mL
1½	CUPS PECANS OR WALNUTS -FINELY CHOPPED	375 mL
1	PINT COFFEE ICE CREAM	500 mL
1	PINT VANILLA ICE CREAM	500 mL

BEAT EGG WHITE WITH SALT UNTIL STIFF. ADD SUGAR GRADUALLY AND FOLD IN NUTS. POUR INTO A WELL-BUTTERED 9" PIE PAN. SPREAD EVENLY ON SIDES AND BOTTOM. PRICK BOTTOM IN 8 OR 10 PLACES. (DO NOT PRICK SIDES.) BAKE AT 400° FOR 10 TO 12 MINUTES. COOL, THEN CHILL. SOFTEN ICE CREAM AND SPREAD ON CRUST. MORE ICE CREAM CAN BE USED IF DESIRED. FREEZE.

CARAMEL SAUCE:

⅔	CUP DARK BROWN SUGAR	150 mL
¼	CUP EVAPORATED MILK	50 mL
¼	CUP BUTTER	50 mL
⅓	CUP LIGHT CORN SYRUP	75 mL
1	EGG YOLK	500 mL
1	TSP. VANILLA	5 mL

MIX ALL INGREDIENTS IN DOUBLE BOILER. COOK 5 MINUTES UNTIL THICKENED. STIR CONSTANTLY. SERVE HOT OVER PIE.

FRUIT DIP

RICH AND WONDERFUL.

1	CUP SOUR CREAM	250 mL
½	PINT WHIPPING CREAM - WHIPPED	250 mL
4	TBSPS. BROWN SUGAR	60 mL
1	TBSP. DARK RUM	15 mL
1	TBSP. GRAND MARNIER	15 mL

MIX TOGETHER AND SERVE WITH SLICED FRUIT AS A DIP OR TOPPING.

FRESH FRUIT DRESSING

LOW CAL - TASTES GREAT RIGHT OUT OF THE JAR!

⅔	CUP PLAIN YOGURT	150 mL
¼	CUP VEGETABLE OIL	50 mL
2	TBSPS. FROZEN ORANGE JUICE CONCENTRATE	30 mL
2	TBSPS. HONEY	30 mL
½	TSP. GRATED ORANGE RIND	2 mL

COMBINE ALL INGREDIENTS AND MIX WELL. REFRIGERATE OVERNIGHT IN A SEALED CONTAINER. MAKES ABOUT 1¼ CUPS.

ENTERTAINING IDEAS:

IT'S TIME FOR A PARTY
WE'RE ALL IN THE MOOD
BUT YOU NEED SOME IDEAS
FOR THE FUN AND THE FOOD

SO WHAT YOU WILL FIND
ON THE PAGES REMAINING
ARE SOME MARVELOUS MENUS
FOR GREAT ENTERTAINING

*INDICATES RECIPES FOUND IN THIS BOOK.

ALSO INCLUDED: RECIPE SUGGESTIONS FROM THE OTHER BOOKS IN 'THE BEST OF BRIDGE' SERIES—

"THE BEST OF BRIDGE"

"ENJOY!"

"WINNERS"

MEXICAN PROGRESSIVE DINNER

A NATURAL FOR THE NEXT NEIGHBOURHOOD NOSH!

<u>MIA CASA</u> – MARGUERITAS MUCHO GRANDÉ ("WINNERS!")
     – COCKTAIL SPREAD *
     – SORTAS *
     – FRESH VEGGIES AND SPRINGTIME
            SPINACH DIP ("WINNERS")

<u>YOURA CASA</u> – ARIZONA FRUIT SALAD *
     – JALAPEÑO CORN STICKS ("WINNERS!")

<u>THEIR A CASA</u> – CHICKEN ENCHILADA CASSEROLE *
     – BURRITOS *
     – COUNTRY CORN BREAD ("WINNERS!")

<u>LASTA CASA</u> – PECAN CRUST ICE CREAM PIE
         WITH CARAMEL SAUCE *
       CHOCOLATE MOUSSE CAKE *

DINNER ALFRESCO

THAT'S A BACKYARD BAR-B-QUE WITH NOISY FRIENDS, INTERESTED NEIGHBOURS AND INSATIABLE INSECTS!

HAM 'N' CHEESE PUFFS *
FRESH VEGGIES AND ZUCCHINI SALAD DIP *
POTLATCH SALMON *
RICE PILAF ("ENJOY!")
A DIFFERENT SPINACH SALAD *
HERB BREAD ("BEST OF BRIDGE")
FRESH FRUIT WITH FRUIT DIP *
BROWNIES ("BEST OF BRIDGE")

POST GAME DINNER

EVEN IF THE TEAM IS LOSING — YOU'RE GOING TO BE A WINNER.

NUTS 'N BOLTS *
CHIPPY KNEES BITES *
SMOKED OYSTER SPREAD *
ASSORTED CRACKERS
SPINACH LASAGNA *
HAM AND MUSHROOM LASAGNA *
TOSSED GREEN SALAD
DRESSED-UP FRENCH BREAD *
ICE BOX PUDDING ("BEST OF BRIDGE")

FOGGY MORNING BRUNCH

THE "MORNING AFTER" RE-HASH. POUR YOUR GUESTS A FUZZY NAVEL AND HAVE A LAUGH!

ROMAINE WITH ORANGES AND PECANS *
QUICHE LORRAINE *
SWISS APPLE QUICHE *
STRAWBERRY BREAD *
FRESH FRUIT TRAY WITH
        FRESH FRUIT DRESSING *
ASSORTED CHEESE TRAY
FUZZY NAVELS *

HOLIDAY HAVOC BUFFET

THE CANDLES ARE FLICKERING -
                    THE SNOW'S ON THE GROUND.
GET READY FOR THE RELATIVES -
                    THEY'RE COMING AROUND.
(OR YOU CAN SPEND ALL THIS TIME AND
MONEY ON YOUR FRIENDS)

UNATTENDED ROAST BEEF (FOR SANDWICHES) *
ASSORTED BREAD AND BUNS
CHEESY MARINATED ONIONS *
CALICO BEANS *
LAYERED SALAD - "ENJOY!"
VEGETABLE SALAD PLATTER - "BEST OF BRIDGE."
BUTTER TART SQUARES *
LEMON BARS - "ENJOY!"
PEANUT BUTTER BROWNIES *

LUNCH FOR THE LADIES

THE LUNCHEON YOU ALWAYS PROMISED TO HAVE.

CHICKEN ASPARAGUS PUFFS. *
THE "LADIES" SEAFOOD CASSEROLE *
RICE
SPINACH SALAD ("BEST OF BRIDGE")
TOFFEE MERINGUE *

HIGH TEA SHOWER

THE BRIDE AND HER FRIENDS ARE HATTED & GLOVED.
YOU ASKED THEM TO TEA-AN IDEA THEY LOVED!
SO GET OUT THE CHINA AND THE GOOD SILVER SERVICE
POISE YOUR PINKIE - YOU NEEDN'T BE NERVOUS!

WELSH CAKES AND SCONES *

     STRAWBERRY JAM
ASPARAGUS SANDWICHES "(BEST OF BRIDGE)"
ASSORTED SANDWICH TRAY
LARGE BOWL, FRESH STRAWBERRIES
FRESH FRUIT 'N' CHEESE TARTS *
LEMON TARTS "(BEST OF BRIDGE)"
WHIPPED SHORTBREAD COOKIES "(BEST OF BRIDGE)"
PECAN TARTS. *

AN OCCASION

SEND OUT THE HAND-LETTERED INVITATIONS—
WE'RE DRESSING FOR DINNER!

SEAFOOD IN WINE *
BASIL AND PARSLEY SOUP *
LEMON SORBET *
BEEF EXTRAORDINAIRE WITH SAUCE DIANE *
OVEN BAKED WILD RICE *
ONION STUFFED BROCCOLI *
DILL AND PARMESAN TOMATOES *
STELLA BY STARLIGHT WITH FRESH BLUEBERRIES
    OR RASPBERRIES *

BRUNCH DISHES

QUICHE - LORRAINE	15
- SWISS APPLE	8
EGGS - OLÉ	12
- FLORENTINE	13
FRENCH TOAST - MIDNIGHT	7
GRILLED CHEESE -	
THE UTMOST	16
SAUSAGE - PIE	10
- 'N JOHNNY CAKE	14

BREADS

BANANA - BEST EVER	21
- BLUEBERRY BANANA	20
BROWN - QUICK MOLASSES	23
CHEESE BUNS - HOW CHEESY	
DO YOU WANT IT?	32
FRENCH - DRESSED-UP	32
PITA TOASTS	31
STRAWBERRY	22
TEA SCONES	34
WELSH CAKES	33

MUFFINS

BANANA	29
CARROT AND RAISIN	27

MUFFINS CONTINUED:

CHEESE AND BACON	28
CREAM CHEESE	24
HEALTH NUT	30
MANDARIN ORANGE	25
RHUBARB - PHANTOM	26

SAUCES & OTHER GOOD THINGS

MARMALADE -	
GREEN TOMATO	38
RELISH:	
CORN	37
PICALILLI	35
SAUCES:	
GOURMET CRANBERRY	38
PEANUT	36
STUFFING:	
TERRIFIC TURKEY	40
CRANBERRY	39
SALT SUBSTITUTE	41
SEASONED FLOUR	41

BEVERAGES

FUZZY NAVELS	43
GLIOGG	42
HOT BUTTERED RUM	43
LONG ISLAND ICED TEA	44
A REAL SMOOTHIE	44

BEST BUFFETS

APPETIZERS

ANTIPASTO - AUNTY LIL'S	
SIMPLE	60
ASPARAGUS - CHICKEN PUFFS	59
BRIE - BRANDY NUT	57
CHEESE - CHIPPY	
KNEES BITES	56
CHICKEN -	
TANGY TIDBITS	61
WINGS, HOT 'N SPICY	55
WINGS, SORTAS	50
COCKTAIL SPREAD	63
CRAB TARTLETS	65
CROUSTADES,	
BOMB SHELTER	48
DILLED OYSTER CRACKERS	56
HAM AND CHEESE PUFFS	64
MUSSEL CREOLE -	
CHEF TONER'S	54
NUTS 'N BOLTS	45
RAREBIT IN A HOLE	46
SALMON PATÉ - EASY	53
SEAFOOD IN WINE	62
SMOKED OYSTER SPREAD	47
SPANAKOPITA	58

SOUPS

AVGOLÉMONO	67
AVOCADO	68
CAULIFLOWER,	
WITH BLUE CHEESE	73
CREAM OF PARSLEY,	
AND BASIL	71
CREAM OF SPINACH	72
MULLIGATAWNY	66
MUSHROOM & LEEK	75
POTATO	74

SALADS

DRESSING -	
CHART HOUSE	
BLEU CHEESE	87
FRESH FRUIT	83
THOUSAND ISLAND	85
BEET SALAD, RUSSIAN	78
COLE SLAW, KILLER	76
FRUIT SALAD, ARIZONA	86
ROMAINE WITH ORANGES	
AND PECANS	80
SPINACH - A DIFFERENT	79
ZUCCHINI SALAD	77

LUNCHEON SALADS

ASPARAGUS PASTA	84
CHICKEN, FRUIT & LIME	88
FRUIT, MARINATED	89
PAPAYA, WITH SHRIMP	
& CURRY MAYONNAISE	81
SALMON PASTA	82

VEGETABLES

ASPARAGUS - BAKED	91
- NOODLE BAKE	92
BANANAS, BAKED IN	
ORANGE & LEMON JUICE	93
BEANS - CALICO POT	94
- SPEEDY BAKED	95
BROCCOLI - SICILIAN	92
- TIMBALES	100
CABBAGE - FRIED	95
CAULIFLOWER - CURRIED	96
ONIONS -	
BROCCOLI STUFFED	106
CHEESE MARINATED	105
PARSNIPS - PERFECT	108
POTATOES -	
FLUFFY BAKED	97
LATKES	107
ROSTI	98

RICE -

OVEN BAKED	111
WILD BUFFET	110
WITH MUSHROOMS	
AND PINE NUTS	109
SPINACH -	
ÉPINARDS, EH?	101
TIMBALES	100
SQUASH -	
SPAGHETTI PRIMAVERA	102
TOMATOES -	
DILL & PARMESAN	99
VIVA VEGGIES	90
ZUCCHINI - ITALIAN	112

BEEF

BEEF EXTRAORDINAIRE	
WITH SAUCE DIANE	118
BURRITOS	113
CABBAGE ROLL CASSEROLE	114
GINGER FRIED BEEF	120
LIVER STIR FRY	119
ROAST BEEF,	
UNATTENDED	123
STROGANOFF -	
SHORT-CUT	116
TACO PIE	115

FISH & SEAFOOD

BAKED FISH MOZZARELLA	127
HALIBUT - WINE POACHED	126
LADIES SEAFOOD CASSEROLE	19
MARINATED FISH FILLETS	
WITH BASIL BUTTER	128
MUSSELS AND SCALLOPS	
IN CREAM	130
SALMON - POTLATCH	129
SALMON STEAKS -	
TERIYAKI	127
SEAFOOD KABOBS	131
SNAPPER - CREAMY DILLED	124
SOLE-O-MIO	125

PORK

HOLY HAM LOAF	161
GREEK RIBS	117
TOMATO CANTONESE	160

FOWL

CHICKEN -	
CATCH-A-TORY	152
CRISPY SESAME	146
ENCHILADA CASSEROLE	153
MANDALAY	154
MEXICANA	159
PARMESAN	149
POT PIE	155
SWEET & SPICY	
CASHEW	148
WHIP LASH	156
CORNISH HENS	150
DUCK BREAST	
EN CASSEROLE	147
PHEASANT -	
ALMOND ORANGE	150

PASTA

BROCCOLI LASAGNA	
AU GRATIN	145
HAM AND MUSHROOM	
LASAGNA	136
SPINACH LASAGNA	143
ITALIAN SAUSAGE & PASTA	132
LINGUINI WITH	
RED CLAM SAUCE	133
MACARONI & CHEESE -	
GOURMET	135
PASTA WITH CRAB	
AND BASIL	134
PASTA PRIMAVERA	138
PENNE - SPICY	142
SPAGHETTI CARBONARA	144

"BADDIES" BUT GOODIES

CANDIES

CHOCOLATE PEANUT

  BUTTER BALLS   171

MICROWAVE PEANUT

        BRITTLE   162

COOKIES

B.L.'S   163

FATAL ATTRACTIONS   168

GINGER SNAPS   169

PEANUT BUTTER   165

PECAN CRISPS   166

POPPY SEED   167

ZUCCHINI   164

SQUARES

BUTTER TART SLICE   172

MATRIMONIAL BARS

  (RHUBARB OR DATE)   170

PEANUT BUTTER BROWNIES   174

PECAN CUPS   177

RHUBARB DELIGHT   181

ROCKY MOUNTAIN

        SQUARES   173

SHORTBREAD TARTS WITH

  CHEESE 'N' FRUIT   178

CAKES

CHOCOLATE MOUSSE   184

DARK CHOCOLATE   191

HAZELNUT TORTE   194

MOCHA WHIPPED CREAM   196

POPPY SEED CHIFFON   192

PUMPKIN CHEESE CAKE   179

DESSERT

CRÉME CARAMEL   188

GRAND SLAM FINALE   187

FROSTY PEACH   180

RHUBARB CRISP WITH

      BOURBON SAUCE   182

SABAYON - CHOCOLATE   189

SABAYON - STELLA

        BY STARLIGHT   193

SORBET - LEMON   190

TIRAMISU   186

TOFFEE MERINGUE   183

PIES

CHOCOLATE PECAN   203

FRENCH LEMON   201

FUDGE WITH

  CUSTARD SAUCE   198

PALACE	200		

PALACE   200

PEACHES & CREAM   197

RHUBARB MERINGUE   204

TIN ROOF   202

PECAN OR WALNUT CRUST

  WITH ICE CREAM &

    CARAMEL SAUCE   205

<u>SAUCES</u>

FRESH FRUIT DRESSING 206

FRUIT DIP   206

YOUR FAVOURITES

Order the Best of Bridge Cookbooks today!
Call our 24-hour toll-free number
1-800-883-4674
or order by using this form.

Please send:

_____ COPIES OF "A YEAR OF THE BEST" — $27.95 ($21.95 US)

_____ COPIES OF "THE BEST OF THE BEST and MORE" — $24.95 ($18.95 US)

_____ COPIES OF "THAT'S TRUMP" — $19.95 ($14.95 US)

_____ COPIES OF "ACES" — $19.95 ($14.95 US)

_____ COPIES OF "GRAND SLAM" — $19.95 ($14.95 US)

_____ COPIES OF "WINNERS" — $19.95 ($14.95 US)

_____ COPIES OF "ENJOY!" — $19.95 ($14.95 US)

_____ COPIES OF "THE BEST OF BRIDGE" — $19.95 ($14.95 US)

_____ Plus $6.00 for first copy postage and handling,
plus $1.00 for each additional copy Canada & US

_____ $15.00 U.S.D. postage and handling for International orders,
plus $1.00 for each additional copy

_____ Add 7% G.S.T. (Canada only). Prices subject to change.

$ _____ is enclosed

NAME: _____

ADDRESS: _____

CITY: _____

PROV./STATE _____ POSTAL/ZIP CODE _____

Charge to ☐ VISA ☐ MASTERCARD ☐ CHEQUE

Account Number: ☐☐☐☐☐☐☐☐☐☐☐☐☐☐☐☐

Expiry Date: ☐☐☐☐

Telephone (in case we have a question about your order): _____

Ship to:

NAME: _____

ADDRESS: _____

CITY: _____

PROV./STATE _____ POSTAL/ZIP CODE _____

The Best of Bridge Publishing Ltd.

6035-6th Street S.E. • Calgary, AB • T2H 1L8 • Tel: (403) 252-0119 • Fax: (403) 252-0206
E-Mail: order@bestofbridge.com • Website: www.bestofbridge.com

The Best of Bridge Cookbook series
over 3,000,000 sold

The Best of Bridge   (The Red Book!)
Full of family favorites: "Herb Bread", "Sweet and Sour Ribs", "Rene's Sandwich Loaf", "Saturday Night Special" and "Icebox Pudding". Best known for an outstanding selection of Christmas baking.

Enjoy!   (The Yellow Book!)
Features a cross section of recipes with a strong focus on appetizers and vegetable dishes. Signature recipes include: "Ham 'N' Cheese Ball", "Fergosa" and "Lemon Pudding". People buy this book just for the "Christmas Morning Wifesaver" recipe!

Winners   (The Green Book!)
Everything from appealing appetizers to delicious desserts. Try "Jalapeño Pepper Jelly", "Chicken Atlanta" and "Pasta Pot". "Spiked Apple Betty" and "Irish Coffee Cream Pie" will be sure-fire hits with your company!

Grand Slam   (The Black Book!)
You'll find a list of menu suggestions for all occasions. Most requested recipes include: "Bomb Shelter Croustades", "Cocktail Spread", "How Cheesy Do You Want It?" and "Teriyaki Salmon Steaks". Serve "Unattended Roast Beef" and "French Lemon Pie" — Entertaining Made Easy!

Aces   (The Blue Book!)
As always, simple recipes with gourmet results! Rave notices for "Peachy Cheese Dip", "Bruschetta", "Major Grey's Meat Loaf" and "Sticky Baked Chicken." "Sour Cream Apple Cake" and "Blueberry Buckle" are kids (big and small!) favorites. Finally — a combined index for the Best of Bridge Series!

That's Trump   (The Dark Green Book!)
Delicious fat-reduced recipes like "Hearty Tortellini Soup" and "Apple Phyllo Crisps'. "Must trys" are: "Muffuletta", "Pork Loin Roast with Apple Topping", "Skor Bar Cookies" and "Easier than Apple Pie". A combined index for the Best of Bridge Series.

The Best of the Best and More   (The BIG Book!)
Over 300 pages, this collection brings together many old favorites and more than 70 new ones. Features 20 color photographs and all new jokes! Still delicious, still familiar ingredients, always "simple recipes with gourmet results".

A Year of the Best   (The Seasons Book)
All new sensational seasonal recipes are enhanced with dozens of luscious full-color photographs. Enjoy the best flavors and the best produce of each season with dishes like Asian Vegetable Rolls, Mango and Spicy Shrimp Salad, Roasted Sweet Potato Wedges, Little Sticky Toffee Puddings.

Order the Best of Bridge Cookbooks today!
Call our 24-hour toll-free number
1-800-883-4674
or order by using this form.

Please send:

_____	COPIES OF "A YEAR OF THE BEST" — $27.95 ($21.95 US)
_____	COPIES OF "THE BEST OF THE BEST and MORE" — $24.95 ($18.95 US)
_____	COPIES OF "THAT'S TRUMP" — $19.95 ($14.95 US)
_____	COPIES OF "ACES" — $19.95 ($14.95 US)
_____	COPIES OF "GRAND SLAM" — $19.95 ($14.95 US)
_____	COPIES OF "WINNERS" — $19.95 ($14.95 US)
_____	COPIES OF "ENJOY!" — $19.95 ($14.95 US)
_____	COPIES OF "THE BEST OF BRIDGE" — $19.95 ($14.95 US)
_____	Plus $6.00 for first copy postage and handling, plus $1.00 for each additional copy Canada & US
_____	$15.00 U.S.D. postage and handling for International orders, plus $1.00 for each additional copy
_____	Add 7% G.S.T. (Canada only). Prices subject to change.
$ _____	is enclosed

NAME: _____

ADDRESS: _____

CITY: _____

PROV./STATE _____ POSTAL/ZIP CODE _____

Charge to   ☐ VISA   ☐ MASTERCARD   ☐ CHEQUE

Account Number: ☐☐☐☐☐☐☐☐☐☐☐☐☐☐☐☐

Expiry Date: ☐☐☐☐

Telephone (in case we have a question about your order): _____

Ship to:

NAME: _____

ADDRESS: _____

CITY: _____

PROV./STATE _____ POSTAL/ZIP CODE _____

The Best of Bridge Publishing Ltd.

6035-6th Street S.E. • Calgary, AB • T2H 1L8 • Tel: (403) 252-0119 • Fax: (403) 252-0206
E-Mail: order@bestofbridge.com • Website: www.bestofbridge.com

The Best of Bridge Cookbook series
over 3,000,000 sold

The Best of Bridge   (The Red Book!)

Full of family favorites: "Herb Bread", "Sweet and Sour Ribs", "Rene's Sandwich Loaf", "Saturday Night Special" and "Icebox Pudding". Best known for an outstanding selection of Christmas baking.

Enjoy!   (The Yellow Book!)

Features a cross section of recipes with a strong focus on appetizers and vegetable dishes. Signature recipes include: "Ham 'N' Cheese Ball", "Fergosa" and "Lemon Pudding". People buy this book just for the "Christmas Morning Wifesaver" recipe!

Winners   (The Green Book!)

Everything from appealing appetizers to delicious desserts. Try "Jalapeño Pepper Jelly", "Chicken Atlanta" and "Pasta Pot". "Spiked Apple Betty" and "Irish Coffee Cream Pie" will be sure-fire hits with your company!

Grand Slam   (The Black Book!)

You'll find a list of menu suggestions for all occasions. Most requested recipes include: "Bomb Shelter Croustades", "Cocktail Spread", "How Cheesy Do You Want It?" and "Teriyaki Salmon Steaks". Serve "Unattended Roast Beef" and "French Lemon Pie" — Entertaining Made Easy!

Aces   (The Blue Book!)

As always, simple recipes with gourmet results! Rave notices for "Peachy Cheese Dip", "Bruschetta", "Major Grey's Meat Loaf" and "Sticky Baked Chicken." "Sour Cream Apple Cake" and "Blueberry Buckle" are kids (big and small!) favorites. Finally — a combined index for the Best of Bridge Series!

That's Trump   (The Dark Green Book!)

Delicious fat-reduced recipes like "Hearty Tortellini Soup" and "Apple Phyllo Crisps'. "Must trys" are: "Muffuletta", "Pork Loin Roast with Apple Topping", "Skor Bar Cookies" and "Easier than Apple Pie". A combined index for the Best of Bridge Series.

The Best of the Best and More   (The BIG Book!)

Over 300 pages, this collection brings together many old favorites and more than 70 new ones. Features 20 color photographs and all new jokes! Still delicious, still familiar ingredients, always "simple recipes with gourmet results".

A Year of the Best   (The Seasons Book)

All new sensational seasonal recipes are enhanced with dozens of luscious full-color photographs. Enjoy the best flavors and the best produce of each season with dishes like Asian Vegetable Rolls, Mango and Spicy Shrimp Salad, Roasted Sweet Potato Wedges, Little Sticky Toffee Puddings.